Modern Application of Drum Ru
With Drum Tabs and Numbers

One Rudiment Per Week

By

Joseph .O. Makanjuola

British Library Cataloguing-in-Publication data

A catalogue record of this book is available from the British Library.

ISBN 978-0-9955421-0-5

© 2016 Joseph .O. Makanjuola, Kent

Joemakanjuola@gmail.com

Printed in the United Kingdom

Disclaimer

The information in this book is meant to supplement, not replace, proper drum training techniques. Like any activity involving speed, sound, equipment, balance and environmental factors, drumming poses some inherent risk. The author and publisher advise readers to take full responsibility for their safety and know their limits. Before practicing the skills described in this book, be sure that your equipment is well maintained. Do not take risks beyond your level of experience, aptitude, training and comfort level.

Foreword

Drumming can be fun, if, first, the drummer has a strong grip of how he or she manages to express his/her self on the instrument effortlessly. To arrive at such a comfortable level means that there has been some substantial amount of time devoted to the art of practicing, and practicing through the right means. The means by which we all learn can be different based on our learning abilities and learning styles.

That said, this book has offered an unorthodox approach to reading drum rudiments - a method that is simplified for the non-traditional music reader for easy understanding and expression on the instrument. This method book contains the key rudiments that are helpful to build strong hands coordination from single strokes to double strokes to paradiddle in an ambidextrous manner, such as right hand lead and left hand. This approach will facilitate a good measure of balance on both hands. It does not end there. The application of basic rock grooves in the book will help to solidify the hand coordination exercises for a well-rounded grip of the drum set, which is an all-limb instrument. Like anything that is worth doing well, to get the best from this book requires time, patience and diligence to work through the details for the right results to manifest.

Tosin Aribisala - Vic firth artist

About the Author

Joseph .O. Makanjuola is a music trainer who started training at age 16. He specialises in training beginner musicians on various instruments, mostly within the gospel genre. His teaching goal is to get beginners to an intermediate level within a ten week period or within a week through an intensive training camp. Due to the numbers of instruments he plays and teaches, he was able to develop drum tabs and the drum number system to aid the development of students with a variety of backgrounds and playing ability especially those with learning difficulties or confidence issues.

Joseph is the pioneer of 'Learn drums in 5 days' which is a successful drum training camp for beginners and intermediate players, which runs at various centres across the year in London, Manchester, Belfast, Essex and Leicester.

He has over 5 years experience working with Special Education Needs Children, both in the secular and gospel scenes.

Introduction

This book is a journey. The first step is to understand the timing of all rudiments. Next will be to apply the information in basic form to an intermediate level through application, all achieved by the end of the year. I recommend the book to be used for a minimum of three years. Within the first year, readers will learn skills that will bridge the gap between not being able to read music to sounding professional in their playing of the drums. The information found in this book can be used by sight readers and professional drummers. The rudiments are in multiple sub-divisions, applied to both hands and feet, each week readers will learn a new rudiment and apply around the drum kit. With knowledge building in mind, basic drum beats will be played to assist the reader transition in and out of the rudiments, which will give the opportunity to apply rudiment learnt. The key features of this book is the ability to expand a basic idea into a minimum of twenty four executions, with unlimited dynamic changes, as per the learners expression. Develop different techniques to enable smoother playing, focus one's time on understanding one rudiment at a time, develop 4-way coordination independence, increase musical vocabulary from an idea, organize thoughts on how to approach fills, develop speed, develop better posture and dexterity, improved sense of timing and dynamics while becoming more musically creative on the drums.

How to use this book

This book covers unique ideas and application methods never seen anywhere. It utilises the concept of drum tabs, rudiment table, dynamic range and drum numbers which are explained in the pages to follow. Each rudiment is introduced via rudiment table that displays how the pattern is laid out. The best approach is to sing each time fragment and play the pattern on the count being sung. Start slow to enable coordination between singing and limbs as well as to maintain accuracy and endurance. The drum numbers provides you with varied options to execute the rudiment pattern being studied. Increase the speed as directed in the brackets. Take regular breaks, pace yourself; three 20 minutes sessions with breaks is more effective than one full hour. Keep an eye on all limbs while practicing to better understand your natural technique and to improve dexterity. If it feels awkward, slow down the pace till the motion feels smooth and natural. Endurance is one of the aim of all exercises, practice them for 20 Minutes or 450 Bars, whichever is shorter.

Keep a record of your progress at the back of the book.

To study the rudiments further, It is advisable to search online on how other drummers or musicians approach the rudiment, no information is useless.

Drum Tabs Guide

Drum tabs is very much similar to the standard music score for drums, the only difference is that each line and space is represented by numbers and symbols rather than music note heads. If you do not understand the timings, just play what you see then speed it up to get the feel.

X represents cymbals, **0** represents the bass drum, **1** is snare drum, **+** sign is ghosted snare and so on as shown in the table below.

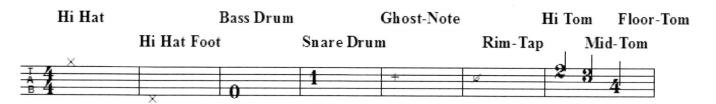

Rudiment Table

The rudiment table is a visual representation of the count / a musical bar. The table displays the layout of the rudiment on a standard music score.

The first row / heading states what type count / time signature being used and applied, for instance, eighth notes. It also represents the length of a musical bar which will be subdivided accordingly .

The second row shows the subdivision of the time signature and how to recite / sing the count as it applies to the rudiment. For instance, eighth note count is:-   **1-and-2-and-3-and-4-and**

The third and forth(where applicable) illustrates the sticking pattern to be used on each count.

	Eighth Note Count Applied						
1	And	2	And	3	And	4	And
L	R	L	R	L	R	L	R

REMEMBER TO VOCALLY SING THE TIMING IN ROW 2 WHILST PLAYING ROW 3.

Dynamic Range

Dynamic range as to be applied to the drum will represent the softest sound we can produce to the loudest sound we can produce on the drums. The Scale we will be using will range from 0 - 10; 0 being pianissimo / practically silent to 10 being fortissimo /the loudest / point of irritation.

0 1 2 3 4 5 6 7 8 9 10

Pianissimo piano   Mezzo forte   Forte   Fortissimo

Drum Numbers

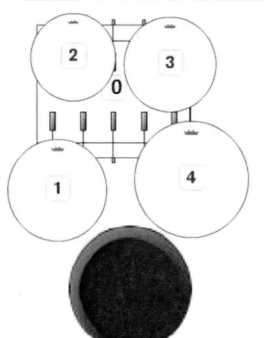

Drum Numbers

Drum Number	Corresponding drum
0	Bass Drum
1	Snare Drum
2	Hi Tom / Tom 1
3	Mid Tom / Tom 2
4	Floor Tom / Tom 3
C	Crash Cymbal
R	Ride Cymbal
X	Closed Hi-hat played with either hand
Y	Hi-hat foot

Contents

16

27

Your success on the drums is connected with your actions, successful drummers keep moving through practice, they make mistakes but they don't quit.

Practice what you hate daily, not just what you know. Your growth depends on it.

Joseph .O. Makanjuola

The Journey Begins.......

Objective - Single Stroke Roll - Left Lead

This week, we aim to achieve a deeper understanding of the single stroke roll.

This rudiment is alternating limbs equally spaced.   Though usually played fast, start off slowly by learning it in quarter note timing before moving on unto eighth note timings.

CONSIDER THE DYNAMIC LEVELS AS **5,** WITH NO CHANGE IN VOLUME.

The pattern is L R L R.

Day 1 - Pattern - L R L R

Quarter Note Hand Tempo = 54 (+8)

TIMING - QUARTER NOTES - COUNTED AS **1 2 3 4**

GUIDE

Quarter Note Count Applied			
1	2	3	4
L	R	L	R

This exercise should be applied on a single surface for now to develop consistency.

THERE IS NO CHANGE IN VOLUME.

Day 2- Pattern - L R L R

Quarter Note Feet Tempo = 54 (+8)

TIMING - QUARTER NOTES - COUNTED AS 1 2 3 4

GUIDE

Quarter Note Count Applied			
1	2	3	4
L	R	L	R

Applied on a single surface, either using Bass drum and Hi-Hat (or double pedal) or your feet rested on the ground, without any hardware.

REMEMBER, THERE IS NO CHANGE IN VOLUME.

Day 3 - Pattern - L R L R

Eighth Note Hand Tempo = 54 (+8)

TIMING - EIGHTH NOTES - COUNTED AS **1 & 2 & 3 & 4 &**

GUIDE

Eighth Note Count Applied							
1	And	2	And	3	And	4	And
L	R	L	R	L	R	L	R

MAINTAIN EQUAL VOLUME THROUGHOUT ESPECIALLY ON BEAT 1.

Day 4 - Pattern - L R L R

Eighth Note Feet Tempo = 54 (+6)
TIMING - EIGHTH NOTES - COUNTED AS 1 & 2 & 3 & 4 &

GUIDE

Eighth Note Count Applied							
1	And	2	And	3	And	4	And
L	R	L	R	L	R	L	R

Maintain equal volume throughout especially on Beat 1. There is a strong possibility your right leg will play accents, Control it.

THERE IS NO CHANGE IN VOLUME.

Day 5 - Pattern - L R L R

Hand Pattern Drum Numbers Tempo = 54 (+8)

TIMING - EIGHTH NOTES - COUNTED AS 1 & 2 & 3 & 4 &

GUIDE

Hand application, an example from the table - 3 1 2 4

Beat 1 + & drum 3 (LR), Beat 2 + & drum 1 (LR),
Beat 3 + & drum 2 (LR), Beat 4 + & drum 4 (LR)

Drum Numbers			
1234	2341	3412	4123
1243	2314	3421	4132
1324	2134	3124	4213
1342	2143	3142	4231
1423	2413	3214	4312
1432	2431	3241	4321

Day 6 - Pattern - L R L R

Hand + Feet Drum Numbers Tempo = 54 (+8)

TIMING - EIGHTH NOTES - COUNTED AS 1 & 2 & 3 & 4 &

GUIDE

Hand application, an example from the table - 3 1 2 4

Beat 1 + & drum 3 (LR), Beat 2 + & drum 1 (LR)
Beat 3 + & drum 2 (LR), Beat 4 + & drum 4 (LR)

BASS DRUM SHOULD PLAY STEADY QUARTER NOTES (1 2 3 4)

Drum Numbers			
1234	2341	3412	4123
1243	2314	3421	4132
1324	2134	3124	4213
1342	2143	3142	4231
1423	2413	3214	4312
1432	2431	3241	4321

Day 7 - Pattern - L R L R

Apply the pattern from day 5 and 6 to the drum beat below.

Always use a metronome at the set tempo. Keep an eye on both hands and feet while practicing to develop better technique and effective posture.

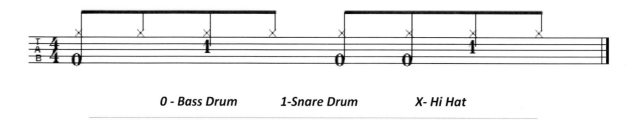

0 - Bass Drum   **1-Snare Drum**   **X- Hi Hat**

Rudiment - Double Stroke Roll - Left Lead

Our aim this week is to develop our left limb as it applies to the double stroke roll. Double stroke is also referred to as diddles.   We will first start by learning it in quarter note timing before moving on unto eighth note timings and finishing off around the kit. All to be applied to our beat of the week.

CONSIDER THE DYNAMIC LEVELS AS 5, WITH NO CHANGE IN VOLUME.

Simply alternate the double strokes on either the hands or feet. The pattern is L L R R.

Day 1 - Pattern - L L R R

Quarter Note Hand Tempo = 54 (+8)
TIMING - QUARTER NOTES - COUNTED AS 1 2 3 4

GUIDE

Quarter Note Count Applied			
1	2	3	4
L	L	R	R

This exercise should be applied on a single surface. This can be either a practice pad or snare drum.
REMEMBER, THERE IS NO CHANGE IN VOLUME.

Day 2- Pattern - L L R R

Quarter Note Feet Tempo = 54 (+8)

TIMING - QUARTER NOTES - COUNTED AS 1 2 3 4

GUIDE

Quarter Note Count Applied			
1	2	3	4
L	L	R	R

Should be Applied on a single surface, either using Bass drum and Hi-Hat (or double pedal) or your feet rested on the ground, without any hardware. **REMEMBER, THERE IS NO CHANGE IN VOLUME.**

Day 3 - Pattern - L L R R

Eighth Note Hand Tempo = 54 (+8)

TIMING - EIGHTH NOTES - COUNTED AS **1 & 2 & 3 & 4 &**

GUIDE

Eighth Note Count Applied							
1	And	2	And	3	And	4	And
L	L	R	R	L	L	R	R

Maintain equal volume throughout especially on Beat 1.

Day 4 - Pattern - L L R R

Eighth Note Feet Tempo = 54 (+6)

TIMING - EIGHTH NOTES - COUNTED AS 1 & 2 & 3 & 4 &

GUIDE

Eighth Note Count Applied							
1	And	2	And	3	And	4	And
L	L	R	R	L	L	R	R

Maintain equal volume throughout especially on Beat 1. There is a strong possibility your right leg will play accents, control it.

REMEMBER, THERE IS NO CHANGE IN VOLUME.

Day 5 - Pattern - L L R R

Hand + Feet Drum Numbers Tempo = 54 (+8)

<u>TIMING - EIGHTH NOTES - COUNTED AS **1 & 2 & 3 & 4 &**</u>

<u>GUIDE</u>

Hand application, an example from the table - 3 1 2 4

Beat 1 + & drum 3 (LL), Beat 2 + & drum 1 (RR),
Beat 3 + & drum 2 (LL), Beat 4 + & drum 4 (RR)

BASS DRUM SHOULD PLAY STEADY QUARTER NOTES (**1 2 3 4**)

Drum Numbers			
1234	2341	3412	4123
1243	2314	3421	4132
1324	2134	3124	4213
1342	2143	3142	4231
1423	2413	3214	4312
1432	2431	3241	4321

Day 6 - Pattern - L L R R

Hand + Feet Drum Numbers Tempo = 54 (+8)

TIMING - EIGHTH NOTES - COUNTED AS 1 & 2 & 3 & 4 &

GUIDE

Hand application, an example from the table - 3 1 2 4

Beat 1 + & drum 3 (LL), Beat 2 + & drum 1 (RR),
Beat 3 + & drum 2 (LL), Beat 4 + & Drum 4 (RR)

BASS DRUM SHOULD PLAY STEADY QUARTER NOTES ON THE OFF BEATS (AND)

Drum Numbers			
1234	2341	3412	4123
1243	2314	3421	4132
1324	2134	3124	4213
1342	2143	3142	4231
1423	2413	3214	4312
1432	2431	3241	4321

Day 7 - Pattern - L L R R

Apply the pattern from day 5 and 6 to the drum beat below.

Always use a metronome at the set tempo. Keep an eye on both hands and feet while practicing to develop better technique and effective posture.

0 - Bass Drum   **1-Snare Drum**   **X- Hi Hat**

Objective - Paradiddle - Right Lead

The most favourite rudiment amongst numerous drummers will be explored from the right limb leading the left. Paradiddle is a mixture of 2 singles and a double.   Paradiddle will be learnt as a rudiment, played as a fill and grooved as a beat.

The first single is accented. The accent makes the sound predictable as well as consistent.

CONSIDER THE DYNAMIC LEVELS AS 6 FOR THE ACCENT AND 3 FOR THE UNACCENTED, WITH NO OTHER CHANGE IN VOLUME.

For a right limb lead, the pattern is **R** L R R followed by **L** R L L.

Day 1 - Pattern - **R** L R R **L** R L L

Quarter Note Hand Tempo = 54 (+8)

TIMING - QUARTER NOTES - COUNTED AS 1 2 3 4

GUIDE

Quarter Note Count Applied			
1	2	3	4
R	L	R	R
L	R	L	L

This exercise should be applied on a single surface for the main time to develop consistency.

REMEMBER, THERE IS AN ACCENT ON BEAT 1 OF BOTH BARS.

Day 2- Pattern - **R** L R R **L** R L L

Quarter Note Feet Tempo = 54 (+8)

TIMING - QUARTER NOTES - COUNTED AS 1 2 3 4

GUIDE

Quarter Note Count Applied			
1	2	3	4
R	L	R	R
L	R	L	L

Should be Applied on a single surface, either using Bass drum and Hi-Hat (or double pedal) or your feet rested on the ground, without any hardware. **REMEMBER, THERE IS AN ACCENT ON BEAT 1 OF BOTH BARS.**

Day 3 - Pattern - **R** L R R **L** R L L

Eighth Note Hand Tempo = 54 (+8)

TIMING - EIGHTH NOTES - COUNTED AS **1 & 2 & 3 & 4 &**

GUIDE

Eighth Note Count Applied							
1	And	2	And	**3**	And	4	And
R	L	R	R	**L**	R	L	L

Maintain equal volume throughout except for Beat 1 and 3 where the accents are.

Day 4 - Pattern - **R** L R R **L** R L L

Eighth Note Feet Tempo = 54 (+6)

TIMING - EIGHTH NOTES - COUNTED AS 1 & 2 & 3 & 4 &

GUIDE

Eighth Note Count Applied							
1	And	**2**	And	**3**	And	**4**	And
R	L	R	R	**L**	R	L	L

Maintain equal volume throughout especially on Beat 1. There is a strong possibility your right leg will play accents, control it.   Accents on beat 1 (Right Leg) and beat 3 (Left Leg).

Day 5 - Pattern - **R** L R R **L** R L L

Hand + Feet Drum Numbers Tempo = 54 (+6)

<u>TIMING - EIGHTH NOTES - COUNTED AS **1 & 2 & 3 & 4 &**</u>

<u>GUIDE</u>

Hand application, an example from the table - 3 1 2 4

Beat 1 + & drum 3 **(R**L), Beat 2 + & drum 1 (RR),
Beat 3 + & drum 2 **(L**R), Beat 4 + & Drum 4 (LL)

BASS DRUM SHOULD PLAY STEADY QUARTER NOTES (1 2 3 4)

Drum Numbers			
1234	2341	3412	4123
1243	2314	3421	4132
1324	2134	3124	4213
1342	2143	3142	4231
1423	2413	3214	4312
1432	2431	3241	4321

Day 6 - Pattern - **R** L R R **L** R L L

Hand + Feet Drum Numbers Tempo = 54 (+8)

<u>TIMING - EIGHTH NOTES - COUNTED AS **1 & 2 & 3 & 4 &**</u>

<u>GUIDE</u>

Hand application, an example from the table - 3 1 2 4

Beat 1 + & drum 3 (**R**L), Beat 2 + & drum 1 (RR),
Beat 3 + & drum 2 (**L**R), Beat 4 + & Drum 4 (LL)

BASS DRUM SHOULD PLAY STEADY QUARTER NOTES ON THE OFF BEATS (AND)

Drum Numbers			
1234	2341	3412	4123
1243	2314	3421	4132
1324	2134	3124	4213
1342	2143	3142	4231
1423	2413	3214	4312
1432	2431	3241	4321

Day 7 - Pattern - **R** L R R **L** R L L

Apply the pattern from day 5 and 6 to the drum beat below.

Always use a metronome at the set tempo. Keep an eye on both hands and feet while practicing to develop better technique and effective posture.

0 - Bass Drum   **1-Snare Drum**   **X- Hi Hat**

Objective - Five Stroke Roll - Left Lead

The first of many rolls to come, five stroke rolls engages 2 double strokes and 1 single.

This week, our left limb will be leading. This is an alternating rudiment.

 The pattern is L L R R **L** followed by R R L L **R**.

<u>CONSIDER THE DYNAMIC LEVELS AS **6** FOR THE ACCENT AND **3** FOR THE UNACCENTED, WITH NO OTHER CHANGE IN VOLUME.</u>

59

Beat of the Week

The drum beat below will support all exercises this week. Always use a metronome at the set tempo. Keep an eye on both hands and feet while practicing to develop better technique and effective posture.

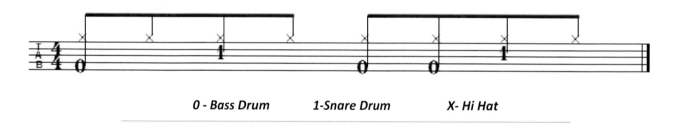

0 - Bass Drum   *1-Snare Drum*   *X- Hi Hat*

Day 1 - Pattern - L L R R **L** R R L L **R**

Eighth Note Hand Tempo = 54 (+8)

TIMING - EIGHTH NOTES - COUNTED AS **1 & 2 & 3 & 4 &**

GUIDE

Eighth Note Count Applied							
1	And	2	And	**3**	**And**	4	And
L	L	R	R	**L**			
R	R	L	L	**R**			

REMEMBER, THE AN ACCENT ON BEAT **3** OF BOTH BARS.

Day 2- Pattern - L L R R **L** R R L L **R**

Eighth Note Feet Tempo = 54 (+6)

TIMING - EIGHTH NOTES - COUNTED AS 1 & 2 & 3 & 4 &

GUIDE

Eighth Note Count Applied							
1	And	2	And	**3**	**And**	4	And
L	L	R	R	**L**			
R	R	L	L	**R**			

REMEMBER, THERE IS AN ACCENT ON BEAT 3 OF BOTH BARS.

Day 3 - Pattern - L L R R **L** R R L L **R**

Sixteenth Note Hand Tempo = 54 (+8)

TIMING - SIXTEENTH NOTES - COUNTED AS 1E &D 2 E & D 3 E & D 4 E & D

GUIDE

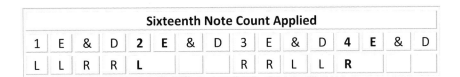

Sixteenth Note Count Applied															
1	E	&	D	2	E	&	D	3	E	&	D	4	E	&	D
L	L	R	R	L				R	R	L	L	R			

Maintain equal volume throughout.

ACCENT IN BOLD.

Day 4 - Pattern - L L R R **L** R R L L **R**

Sixteenth Note Feet Tempo = 44 (+6)

TIMING - SIXTEENTH NOTES - COUNTED AS 1E &D 2 E & D 3 E & D 4 E & D

GUIDE

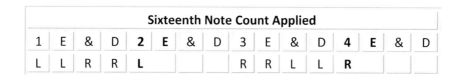

Sixteenth Note Count Applied															
1	E	&	D	**2**	**E**	&	D	3	E	&	D	**4**	**E**	&	D
L	L	R	R	**L**				R	R	L	L	**R**			

Maintain equal volume throughout.

ACCENT IN BOLD.

Day 5 - Pattern - L L R R **L** R R L L **R**

Split Hand & Feet Drum Numbers Tempo = 54 (+8)
Timing - Sixteenth Notes - Counted as 1E &D 2 E & D 3 E & D 4 E & D

Guide

Today's task is to split the limb.

- Play the left hand with the right leg **(HHLLH)**
- Play the left leg with the right hand **(LLHHL)**

Drum Numbers			
123	234	341	412
124	231	342	413
132	213	312	421
134	214	314	423
142	241	321	431
143	243	324	432

Day 6 - Pattern - L L R R **L** R R L L **R**

Split Hand &Feet Drum Numbers Tempo = 54 (+8)
Timing - Sixteenth Notes - Counted as 1e &d 2 e & d 3 e & d 4 e & d

Guide

Today's task is similar to yesterday, the difference is we are Incorporating the hi-hat.

- Play the left hand with the right leg **(HHLLH)**
- Play the left leg with the right hand **(LLHHL)**

Drum Numbers			
12X	2X 4	X 41	412
124	2X 1	X 42	41X
1X 2	21X	X 12	421
1X 4	214	X 14	42X
142	241	X 21	4X 1
14X	24X	X 24	4X 2

Day 7 - Pattern - L L R R **L** R R L L **R**

Hand + Feet Drum Numbers Tempo = 54 (+8)

TIMING - SIXTEENTH NOTES - COUNTED AS 1E &D 2 E & D 3 E & D 4 E & D

GUIDE

Example of Hand Drum Numbers Applied			
2	1	X	4
(R) LLRR	**L** RR LL	**R** LL RR	**L** RR LL

THE (R) IS TO FINISH THE RIGHT HAND ROLL THAT STARTED ON DRUM **4**

BASS DRUM SHOULD PLAY STEADY QUARTER NOTES

Drum Numbers			
12X4	2X41	X412	412X
124X	2X14	X421	41X2
1X24	21X4	X124	421X
1X42	214X	X142	42X1
142X	241X	X214	4X12
14X2	24X1	X241	4X21

Objective - Double Stroke - Right Lead

Our aim this week is to develop our left limb as it applies to the double stroke roll. We will continue what we learnt in quarter note timing by moving on to eighth note timings and finishing off with sixteenth note timing. All to be applied to our beat of the week.

Simply alternating double strokes of either the hand or feet. The pattern is R R L L.

CONSIDER THE DYNAMIC LEVELS AS 5, WITH NO CHANGE IN VOLUME.

Beat of the Week

The drum beat below will support all exercises this week. Always use a metronome at the set tempo. Keep an eye on both hands and feet while practicing to develop better technique and effective posture.

0 - Bass Drum   **1-Snare Drum**   **X- Hi Hat**

Day 1 - Pattern - R R L L

Eighth Note Hand Tempo = 54 (+8)

TIMING - EIGHTH NOTES - COUNTED AS 1 & 2 & 3 & 4 &

GUIDE

Eighth Note Count Applied							
1	And	2	And	3	And	4	And
R	R	L	L	R	R	L	L

REMEMBER, THERE IS NO ACCENT.

Day 2- Pattern - R R L L

Eighth Note Feet Tempo = 54 (+6)

TIMING - EIGHTH NOTES - COUNTED AS **1 & 2 & 3 & 4 &**

GUIDE

Eighth Note Count Applied							
1	And	2	And	3	And	4	And
R	R	L	L	R	R	L	L

REMEMBER, THERE IS NO ACCENT.

Day 3 - Pattern - R R L L

Sixteenth Note Hand Tempo = 54 (+8)

TIMING - SIXTEENTH NOTES - COUNTED AS 1E &D 2 E & D 3 E & D 4 E & D

GUIDE

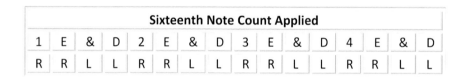

Sixteenth Note Count Applied															
1	E	&	D	2	E	&	D	3	E	&	D	4	E	&	D
R	R	L	L	R	R	L	L	R	R	L	L	R	R	L	L

REMEMBER, THERE IS NO ACCENT.

Day 4 - Pattern - R R L L

Sixteenth Note Feet Tempo = 34 (+6)

TIMING - SIXTEENTH NOTES - COUNTED AS 1E &D 2 E & D 3 E & D 4 E & D

GUIDE

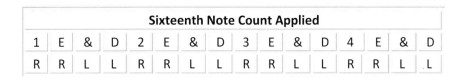

Sixteenth Note Count Applied															
1	E	&	D	2	E	&	D	3	E	&	D	4	E	&	D
R	R	L	L	R	R	L	L	R	R	L	L	R	R	L	L

REMEMBER, THERE IS NO ACCENT.

Day 5 - Pattern - R R L L

Hand + Feet Drum Numbers Tempo = 54 (+8)

<u>TIMING - SIXTEENTH NOTES - COUNTED AS 1E &D 2 E & D 3 E & D 4 E & D</u>

<u>GUIDE</u>

Hand application, an example from the table - 3 1 2 4

Example of Hand Drum Numbers Applied			
3	1	2	4
RRLL	RRLL	RRLL	RRLL

<u>BASS DRUM SHOULD PLAY STEADY QUARTER NOTES (1 2 3 4)</u>

Hand Drum Numbers			
1234	2341	3412	4123
1243	2314	3421	4132
1324	2134	3124	4213
1342	2143	3142	4231
1423	2413	3214	4312
1432	2431	3241	4321

Day 6 - Pattern - R R L L

Split Hand + Feet Drum Numbers Tempo = 54 (+8)

TIMING - SIXTEENTH NOTES - COUNTED AS 1E &D 2 E & D 3 E & D 4 E & D

GUIDE

- Play the left hand with the right leg **(HHLL)**
- Play the left leg with the right hand **(LLHH)**

Hand Drum Numbers			
1234	2341	3412	4123
1243	2314	3421	4132
1324	2134	3124	4213
1342	2143	3142	4231
1423	2413	3214	4312
1432	2431	3241	4321

Day 7 - Pattern - R R L L

Eighth Note Triplet Hand + Feet Tempo = 44 (+8)

TIMING - EIGHTH NOTE TRIPLET - COUNTED AS 1 TRIP LET 2 TRIP LET 3 TRIP LET 4 TRIP LET

GUIDE

Eighth Note triplet Count											
1	Trip	Let	2	Trip	Let	3	Trip	Let	4	Trip	Let
R	R	L	L	R	R	L	L	R	R	L	L

- PATTERN SHOULD BE PLAYED ON A SINGLE SURFACE WHILE BASS DRUM SHOULD PLAY STEADY QUARTER NOTES
- ONCE YOU ARE COMFORTABLE WITH THIS EXERCISE ON A SINGLE SURFACE, APPLY TO THE BEAT OF THE WEEK.

Objective - Inverted Double Stroke 1 - Left

This week we will be exploring the double stroke again, however we will be inverting the pattern from the regular R R L L or L L R R.

As usual, we will first start by learning it in quarter note timing before moving on unto eighth note timings and finishing off with sixteenth note times. All to be applied to our beat of the week.

<u>CONSIDER THE DYNAMIC LEVELS AS **5**, WITH NO CHANGE IN VOLUME.</u>

The inverted double stroke roll pattern we will be exploring is L R R L.

Beat of the Week

The drum beat below will support all exercises this week. Always use a metronome at the set tempo. Keep an eye on both hands and feet while practicing to develop better technique and effective posture.

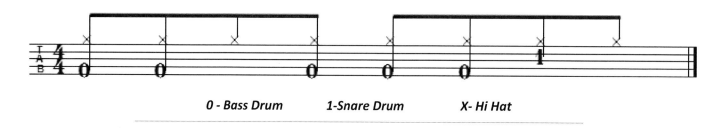

0 - Bass Drum   *1-Snare Drum*   *X- Hi Hat*

Day 1 - Pattern - L R R L

Eighth Note Hand Tempo = 54 (+8)

TIMING - EIGHTH NOTES - COUNTED AS **1 & 2 & 3 & 4 &**

GUIDE

Eighth Note Count Applied							
1	And	2	And	3	And	4	And
L	R	R	L	L	R	R	L

REMEMBER, THERE IS NO ACCENT.

Day 2- Pattern - L R R L

Eighth Note Feet Tempo = 54 (+6)

TIMING - EIGHTH NOTES - COUNTED AS 1 & 2 & 3 & 4 &

GUIDE

Eighth Note Count Applied							
1	And	2	And	3	And	4	And
L	R	R	L	L	R	R	L

REMEMBER, THERE IS NO ACCENT.

Day 3 - Pattern - L R R L

Sixteenth Note Hand Tempo = 54 (+8)

TIMING - SIXTEENTH NOTES - COUNTED AS 1E &D 2 E & D 3 E & D 4 E & D

GUIDE

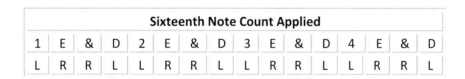

Sixteenth Note Count Applied															
1	E	&	D	2	E	&	D	3	E	&	D	4	E	&	D
L	R	R	L	L	R	R	L	L	R	R	L	L	R	R	L

REMEMBER, THERE IS NO ACCENT.

Day 4 - Pattern - L R R L

Sixteenth Note Feet Tempo = 34 (+6)

TIMING - SIXTEENTH NOTES - COUNTED AS 1E &D 2 E & D 3 E & D 4 E & D

GUIDE

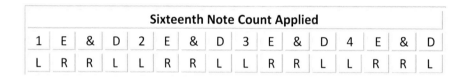

Sixteenth Note Count Applied															
1	E	&	D	2	E	&	D	3	E	&	D	4	E	&	D
L	R	R	L	L	R	R	L	L	R	R	L	L	R	R	L

REMEMBER, THERE IS NO ACCENT.

Day 5 - Pattern - L R R L

Hand + Feet Drum Numbers Tempo = 54 (+8)

TIMING - SIXTEENTH NOTES - COUNTED AS 1E &D 2 E & D 3 E & D 4 E & D

GUIDE

Hand application, an example from the table - 3 1 2 4

Example of Hand Drum Numbers Applied			
3	1	2	4
LRRL	LRRL	LRRL	LRRL

BASS DRUM SHOULD PLAY STEADY QUARTER NOTES (1 2 3 4)

Hand Drum Numbers			
1234	2341	3412	4123
1243	2314	3421	4132
1324	2134	3124	4213
1342	2143	3142	4231
1423	2413	3214	4312
1432	2431	3241	4321

Day 6 - Pattern - L R R L

Split Hand + Feet D.Numbers Tempo = 54 (+8)

TIMING - SIXTEENTH NOTES - COUNTED AS 1E &D 2 E & D 3 E & D 4 E & D

GUIDE

- Play the left hand with the right foot (HHLL)
- Play the left Feet with the right hand (LLHH)

Hand Drum Numbers			
1234	2341	3412	4123
1243	2314	3421	4132
1324	2134	3124	4213
1342	2143	3142	4231
1423	2413	3214	4312
1432	2431	3241	4321

Day 7 - Pattern - L R R L

Unison Hand and Feet Tempo = 54 (+8)

TIMING - SIXTEENTH NOTES - COUNTED AS 1E &D 2 E & D 3 E & D 4 E & D

GUIDE

TODAY'S EXERCISE IS STRAIGHTFORWARD, ALL YOU ARE TO DO IS TO PLAY THE HANDS AND FEET IN UNISON. IT IS SIMPLY LEFT FOOT + LEFT HAND TOGETHER AND RIGHT FOOT + RIGHT HAND TOGETHER.

ONCE YOU ARE COMFORTABLE WITH THE EXERCISE, APPLY TO THE HAND DRUM NUMBERS ACROSS THE KIT

Objective - Single Stroke 4 - Right Lead

This is the first of our triplet based rudiments.   Single stroke 4 is alternating singles similar to the single stroke roll, the difference is the timing. We will first start by learning it in eighth note triplet timing and finishing off with sixteenth note triplet timing.

The pattern for a right limb lead is R L R **L**

CONSIDER THE DYNAMIC LEVELS AS **6** FOR THE ACCENT AND **3** FOR THE UNACCENTED, WITH NO OTHER CHANGE IN VOLUME.

86

Beat of the Week

The drum beat below will support all exercises this week. Always use a metronome at the set tempo. Keep an eye on both hands and feet while practicing to develop better technique and effective posture.

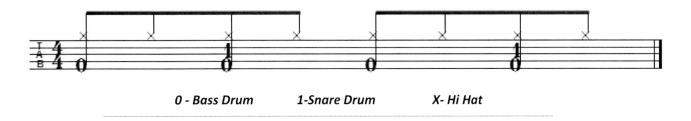

0 - Bass Drum   **1-Snare Drum**   **X- Hi Hat**

Day 1 - Pattern - R L R **L**

Eighth Note Triplet Hand Tempo = 54 (+8)

TIMING - EIGHTH NOTES TRIPLET - COUNTED AS 1 TRIP LET 2 TRIP LET 3 TRIP LET 4 TRIP LET

GUIDE

Eighth Note triplet Count											
1	Trip	Let	**2**	**Trip**	**Let**	3	Trip	Let	**4**	**Trip**	**Let**
R	L	R	**L**			R	L	R	**L**		

REMEMBER, ACCENTS ARE ON **2** AND **4**

Day 2- Pattern - R L R **L**

Eighth Note Triplet Feet Tempo = 44 (+6)

TIMING - EIGHTH NOTES TRIPLET - COUNTED AS 1 TRIP LET 2 TRIP LET 3 TRIP LET 4 TRIP LET

GUIDE

Eighth Note triplet Count											
1	Trip	Let	**2**	**Trip**	**Let**	3	Trip	Let	**4**	**Trip**	**Let**
R	L	R	**L**			R	L	R	**L**		

REMEMBER, ACCENTS ARE ON 2 AND 4

Day 3 - Pattern - R L R **L**

Pattern as a Beat Tempo = 54 (+8)

TIMING - EIGHTH NOTES TRIPLET - COUNTED AS 1 TRIP LET 2 TRIP LET 3 TRIP LET 4 TRIP LET

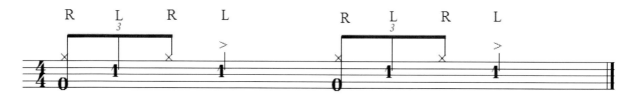

FOR THIS RUDIMENT TO WORK AS A BEAT, MAINTAIN THE TIMINGS AS WRITTEN. ONCE COMFORTABLE, PLAY THE BEAT OF THE WEEK THEN APPLY ABOVE PATTERN AS A DRUM FILL.

ACCENTS ARE ON 2 AND 4

Day 4 - Pattern - R L R **L**

Pattern as a Beat Tempo = 54 (+8)

TIMING - EIGHTH NOTES TRIPLET - COUNTED AS 1 TRIP LET 2 TRIP LET 3 TRIP LET 4 TRIP LET

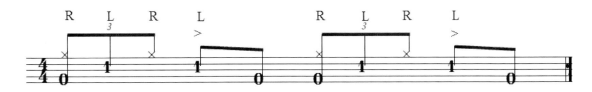

FOR THIS RUDIMENT TO WORK AS A BEAT, MAINTAIN THE TIMINGS AS WRITTEN. ONCE COMFORTABLE, PLAY THE BEAT OF THE WEEK THEN APPLY ABOVE PATTERN AS A DRUM FILL.

ACCENTS ARE ON **2** AND **4**

Day 5 - Pattern - R L R **L**

Sixteenth Note Triplet Hand Tempo = 54 (+8)

TIMING - SIXTEENTH NOTES TRIPLET - COUNTED AS

1 TRIP LET AND TRIP LET 2 TRIP LET AND TRIP LET 3 TRIP LET AND TRIP LET 4 TRIP LET AND TRIP LET

GUIDE

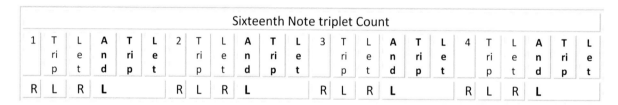

Sixteenth Note triplet Count																							
1	T ri p	L e t	A n d	T ri p	L e t	2	T ri p	L e t	A n d	T ri p	L e t	3	T ri p	L e t	A n d	T ri p	L e t	4	T ri p	L e t	A n d	T ri p	L e t
R	L	R	**L**				R	L	R	**L**			R	L	R	**L**			R	L	R	**L**	

BASS DRUM SHOULD PLAY STEADY QUARTER NOTES (1 2 3 4)

92

Day 6 - Pattern - R L R **L**

Sixteenth Note Triplet Feet Tempo = 34 (+6)

<u>TIMING - SIXTEENTH NOTES TRIPLET - COUNTED AS</u>

<u>1 TRIP LET AND TRIP LET 2 TRIP LET AND TRIP LET 3 TRIP LET AND TRIP LET 4 TRIP LET AND TRIP LET</u>

<u>GUIDE</u>

Sixteenth Note triplet Count																							
1	T rip	L e t	A n d	T rip	L e t	2	T rip	L e t	A n d	T rip	L e t	3	T rip	L e t	A n d	T rip	L e t	4	T rip	L e t	A n d	T rip	L e t
R	L	R	**L**			R	L	R	**L**			R	L	R	**L**			R	L	R	**L**		

<u>BASS DRUM SHOULD PLAY STEADY QUARTER NOTES (1 2 3 4)</u>

93

Day 7 - Pattern - R L R **L**

Unison Hand and Feet Tempo = 54 (+8)

TIMING - SIXTEENTH NOTES TRIPLET - COUNTED AS   1 TRIP LET AND TRIP LET 2 TRIP LET AND TRIP LET 3 TRIP LET AND TRIP LET 4 TRIP LET AND TRIP LET

GUIDE

APPLY DAY 5 EXERCISES TO THE NUMBERS ACROSS THE DRUM KIT.

SPEED IS NOT OUR GOAL, ACCURACY IS.

Hand Drum Numbers			
12X4	2X41	X412	412X
124X	2X14	X421	41X2
1X24	21X4	X124	421X
1X42	214X	X142	42X1
142X	241X	X214	4X12
14X2	24X1	X241	4X21

Objective - Single Stroke 7 - Left Lead

Another of our triplet based rudiment is the single stroke 7. As a rudiment, it is made up of alternating single strokes that ends on the starting limb. We will first start by learning it in quarter note timing before moving on unto eighth note timings and finishing off with sixteenth note timing. We will be learning the single stroke 7 from a left hand lead perceptive. This is an alternating rudiment.

<u>CONSIDER THE DYNAMIC LEVELS AS **6** FOR THE ACCENT AND **3** FOR THE UNACCENTED, WITH NO OTHER CHANGE IN VOLUME.</u>

The pattern is L R L R L R **L**. R L R L R L **R**

Beat of the Week

The drum beat will support all exercises this week. Always use a metronome at the set tempo. Keep an eye on both hands and feet while practicing to develop better technique and effective posture.

0 - Bass Drum   1-Snare Drum   X- Hi Hat

Day 1 - Pattern - L R L R L R **L**   R L R L R L **R**

Eighth Note Triplet Hand Tempo = 54 (+8)

TIMING - EIGHTH NOTES TRIPLET - COUNTED AS 1 TRIP LET 2 TRIP LET 3 TRIP LET 4 TRIP LET

GUIDE

Eighth Note triplet Count											
1	Trip	Let	2	Trip	Let	**3**	Trip	Let	4	Trip	Let
L	R	L	R	L	R	**L**					
R	L	R	L	R	L	**R**					

Play this exercise as a two bar alternating pattern.

ACCENT IS ON 3

Day 2- Pattern - L R L R L R **L** R L R L R L **R**

Eighth Note Triplet Feet Tempo = 44 (+6)

TIMING - EIGHTH NOTES TRIPLET - COUNTED AS 1 TRIP LET 2 TRIP LET 3 TRIP LET 4 TRIP LET

GUIDE

Eighth Note triplet Count											
1	Trip	Let	2	Trip	Let	**3**	Trip	Let	4	Trip	Let
L	R	L	R	L	R	**L**					
R	L	R	L	R	L	**R**					

REMEMBER, ACCENT IS ON **3**

Day 3 - Pattern - L R L R L R **L**   R L R L R L **R**

Hand D.Numbers Tempo = 54 (+8)

<u>TIMING - EIGHTH NOTES TRIPLET - COUNTED AS 1 TRIP LET 2 TRIP LET 3 TRIP LET 4 TRIP LET</u>

<u>GUIDE</u>

Hand application, an example from the table - 3 1 2 4

Bar 1 (LRLRLR**L**) gets drum 3, Bar 2 (RLRLRL**R**) gets drum 1,

Bar 3 (LRLRLR**L**) gets drum 2, Bar 4 (RLRLRL**R**) gets drum 4

<u>THIS IS A 4 BAR PATTERN</u>

Drum Numbers			
1234	2341	3412	4123
1243	2314	3421	4132
1324	2134	3124	4213
1342	2143	3142	4231
1423	2413	3214	4312
1432	2431	3241	4321

Day 4 - Pattern - L R L R L R **L** R L R L R L **R**

Split Hand and Feet Tempo = 54 (+8)

TIMING - EIGHTH NOTES TRIPLET - COUNTED AS 1 TRIP LET 2 TRIP LET 3 TRIP LET 4 TRIP LET

GUIDE

Today's task is to split the limbs.

- Play the left hand with the right leg **(HHLLH)**
- Play the left leg with the right hand **(LLHHL)**
- Alternate between exercise 1 and 2

Day 5 - Pattern - L R L R L R **L** R L R L R L **R**

Unison Hand and Feet Tempo = 54 (+4)

TIMING - EIGHTH NOTES TRIPLET - COUNTED AS 1 TRIP LET 2 TRIP LET 3 TRIP LET 4 TRIP LET

GUIDE

Today's task is to unite the limbs.

- Play the left hand and Left Foot together, whilst Right hand and Right Foot played together within the pattern

Day 6 - Pattern - L R L R L R **L**   R L R L R L **R**

Feet incorporated with Hand Tempo = 54 (+6)

TIMING - EIGHTH NOTES TRIPLET - COUNTED AS 1 TRIP LET 2 TRIP LET 3 TRIP LET 4 TRIP LET

GUIDE

Eighth Note triplet Count											
1	Trip	Let	2	Trip	Let	**3**	Trip	Let	4	Trip	Let
L	R	L	R	L	R	**L**	0	0			
R	L	R	L	R	L	**R**	0	0			

0 = BASS DRUM

ACCENTS ARE ON 3

102

Day 7 - Pattern - L R L R L R **L**   R L R L R L **R**

Unison Hand + Feet Tempo = 54 (+6)

TIMING - SIXTEENTH NOTES TRIPLET - COUNTED AS 1 TRIP LET AND TRIP LET 2 TRIP LET AND TRIP LET 3 TRIP LET AND TRIP LET 4 TRIP LET AND TRIP LET

GUIDE

TODAY'S EXERCISE IS QUITE STRAIGHTFORWARD. APPLY YESTERDAY'S EXERCISES TO THE HAND DRUM NUMBERS TO GET COMFORTABLE ACROSS THE KIT

SPEED IS NOT OUR GOAL, ACCURACY WITH EASE IS THE MAIN GOAL.

Hand Drum Numbers			
1234	2341	3412	4123
1243	2314	3421	4132
1324	2134	3124	4213
1342	2143	3142	4231
1423	2413	3214	4312
1432	2431	3241	4321

Objective - 10 Stroke Roll - Right Lead

The ten stroke roll consists of 4 doubles and 2 singles. The doubles are twice as fast as the singles. We will be learning it in sixteenth note timing.   This is an alternating rudiment.

CONSIDER THE DYNAMIC LEVELS AS 6 FOR THE ACCENT AND 3 FOR THE UNACCENTED, WITH NO OTHER CHANGE IN VOLUME.

The pattern for the 10 stroke roll right lead is R R L L R R L L **R L**.

Beat of the Week

The drum beat will support all exercises this week. Always use a metronome at the set tempo. Keep an eye on both hands and feet while practicing to develop better technique and effective posture.

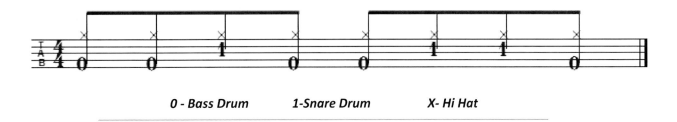

0 - Bass Drum   1-Snare Drum   X- Hi Hat

Day 1- Pattern - RRLLRRLL**RL** LLRRLLRR**LR**

Sixteenth Note Hand Tempo = 54 (+8)

TIMING - SIXTEENTH NOTES - COUNTED AS 1E &D 2 E & D 3 E & D 4 E & D

GUIDE

Sixteenth Note Count Applied															
1	E	&	D	2	E	&	D	**3**	E	**&**	D	4	E	&	D
R	R	L	L	R	R	L	L	**R**		L					
L	L	R	R	L	L	R	R	**L**		R					

Play this exercise as a two bar alternating pattern.

ACCENTS ARE ON 3 + AND

Day 2- Pattern - RRLLRRLL**RL** LLRRLLRR**LR**

Sixteenth Note Feet Tempo = 34 (+6)

TIMING - SIXTEENTH NOTES - COUNTED AS 1E &D 2 E & D 3 E & D 4 E & D

GUIDE

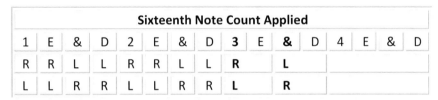

Sixteenth Note Count Applied															
1	E	&	D	2	E	&	D	**3**	E	**&**	D	4	E	&	D
R	R	L	L	R	R	L	L	**R**		**L**					
L	L	R	R	L	L	R	R	**L**		**R**					

Play this exercise as a two bar alternating pattern.

ACCENTS ARE ON 3 + AND

Day 3- Pattern - RRLLRRLL**RL** LLRRLLRR**LR**

Full Pattern Hand D.Numbers Tempo = 54 (+8)

TIMING - SIXTEENTH NOTES - COUNTED AS 1E &D 2 E & D 3 E & D 4 E & D

GUIDE

Hand application, an example from the table - 3 1 2 4

Bar 1 (RRLLRRLL**RL**) gets drum 3, Bar 2 (LLRRLLRR**LR**) gets drum 1,
Bar 3 (RRLLRRLL**RL**) gets drum 2, Bar 4 (LLRRLLRR**LR**) gets drum 4

BASS DRUM SHOULD HAVE STEADY QUARTER NOTE PULSE.

MAINTAIN ACCENTS ARE ON 3 + AND

Drum Numbers			
1234	2341	3412	4123
1243	2314	3421	4132
1324	2134	3124	4213
1342	2143	3142	4231
1423	2413	3214	4312
1432	2431	3241	4321

Day 4- Pattern - RRLLRRLL**RL** LLRRLLRR**LR**

Hi-Hat Hand Tempo = 54 (+8)

TIMING - SIXTEENTH NOTES - COUNTED AS 1E &D 2 E & D 3 E & D 4 E & D

GUIDE

Play the rudimental pattern on the Hi-hat firmly closed, whilst playing steady quarter notes on the bass drum. Start slow making sure the accents are correctly placed.

BASS DRUM SHOULD HAVE STEADY QUARTER NOTE PULSE.

MAINTAIN ACCENTS ARE ON 3 + AND

Day 5- Pattern - RRLLRRLL**RL** LLRRLLRR**LR**

Split Hand + Feet Tempo = 54 (+6)

<u>TIMING - SIXTEENTH NOTES - COUNTED AS 1E &D 2 E & D 3 E & D 4 E & D</u>

<u>GUIDE</u>

Today's task is to split the limbs.

- Play the Right hand with the left leg **(HHLLHHLLHL)**
- Play the Right leg with the right hand **(LLHHLLHHLH)**
- Alternate between exercise 1 and 2

Day 6- Pattern - RRLLRRLL**RL** LLRRLLRR**LR**

Split Hand D.Numbers Tempo = 54 (+8)

TIMING - SIXTEENTH NOTES - COUNTED AS 1E &D 2 E & D 3 E & D 4 E & D

GUIDE

Hand application, an example from the table - 1 2 3 4

Bar 1 - Drum 1 (RRLL) Drum 2 (RRLL) Drum 3 **(R)** Drum 4 **(L)**

Bar 2 - Drum 1 (LLRR) Drum 2 (LLRR) Drum 3 **(L)** Drum 4 **(R)**

ACCENTS ARE ON **3 + A**ND

Hand Drum Numbers			
1234	2341	3412	4123
1243	2314	3421	4132
1324	2134	3124	4213
1342	2143	3142	4231
1423	2413	3214	4312
1432	2431	3241	4321

Day 7 - Pattern - RRLLRRLL**RL** LLRRLLRR**LR**

Split Hand D.Numbers Tempo = 54 (+8)

<u>Timing - Sixteenth Notes - Counted as 1e &d 2 e & d 3 e & d 4 e & d</u>

<u>Guide</u>

Same as yesterdays, but with quarter notes on bass drum and the crash cymbal on beat 1 as we return to the drum beat.

<u>Bass drum should have steady quarter note pulse. Play the crash cymbal on beat 1 to begin drum beat.</u>

Accents are on 3 + And

Hand Drum Numbers			
1234	2341	3412	4123
1243	2314	3421	4132
1324	2134	3124	4213
1342	2143	3142	4231
1423	2413	3214	4312
1432	2431	3241	4321

Objective - Inverted Paradiddle 1 -Right Lead

The Paradiddle pattern is **R** L R R **L** R L L. The inverted Paradiddle we will be exploring is the **R** L L **R** L R R **L**. Another name for given to this method of Paradiddle is Radiddlepa. This week's approach to the Paradiddle will have a more unique perceptive especially as we apply on the drums to create different fills and a beat.   We will learn it in eighth note timing (see below) and finish off with sixteenth note timing as a beat.

CONSIDER THE DYNAMIC LEVELS AS **6** FOR THE ACCENT AND **3** FOR THE UNACCENTED, WITH NO OTHER CHANGE IN VOLUME.

 The pattern again is **R** L L **R** L R R **L**.

Beat of the Week

The drum beat will support all exercises this week. Always use a metronome at the set tempo. Keep an eye on both hands and feet while practicing to develop better technique and effective posture.

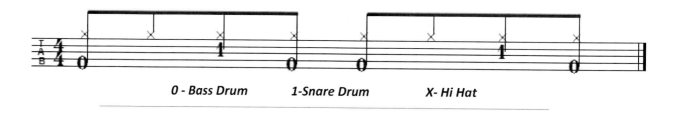

0 - Bass Drum   1-Snare Drum   X- Hi Hat

Day 1- Pattern - **R** L L **R** **L** R R **L**

Eighth Note Hand Tempo = 54 (+8)

TIMING - EIGHTH NOTES - COUNTED AS 1 & 2 & 3 & 4 &

GUIDE

Eighth Note Count Applied							
1	And	2	**And**	3	And	4	**And**
R	L	L	R	L	R	R	L

ACCENTS ARE ON 1 + AND OF 2 + 3 + AND OF 4

Day 2- Pattern - **R** L L **R L** R R **L**

Eighth Note Feet Tempo = 54 (+6)

<u>TIMING - EIGHTH NOTES - COUNTED AS 1 & 2 & 3 & 4 &</u>

<u>GUIDE</u>

Eighth Note Count Applied							
1	And	2	**And**	**3**	And	4	**And**
R	L	L	R	L	R	R	L

<u>ACCENTS ARE ON **1** + AND **OF 2** + **3** + AND OF **4**</u>

Day 3- Pattern - **R** L L **R** L R R **L**

Hand D.Numbers Tempo = 54 (+8)

TIMING - EIGHTH NOTES - COUNTED AS **1 & 2 & 3 & 4 &**

GUIDE

Hand application, an example from the table - 3 1 2 4

Beat 1 + & gets drum 3 (**R**L), Beat 2 + & gets drum 1 (L**R**), Beat 3 + & gets drum 2(L**R**), Beat 4 + & gets Drum 4 (**R**L)

BASS DRUM SHOULD HAVE STEADY QUARTER NOTE PULSE.

ALSO ACCENTS ARE ON **1** + AND **OF 2 +** 3 + AND OF **4**

Drum Numbers			
1234	2341	3412	4123
1243	2314	3421	4132
1324	2134	3124	4213
1342	2143	3142	4231
1423	2413	3214	4312
1432	2431	3241	4321

Day 4- Pattern - **R** L L **R** L R R **L**

Split Hand + Feet Tempo = 54 (+8)

TIMING - EIGHTH NOTES - COUNTED AS **1 & 2 & 3 & 4 &**

GUIDE

Today's task is to split the limb.

- Play the Right hand with the Left leg (**HLLHLHHL**)
- Play the Right leg with the left hand (**LHHLHLLH**)

Hand Drum Numbers			
1234	2341	3412	4123
1243	2314	3421	4132
1324	2134	3124	4213
1342	2143	3142	4231
1423	2413	3214	4312
1432	2431	3241	4321

Day 5- Pattern - **R** L L **R L** R R **L**

Pattern as a Beat Tempo = 54 (+8)

TIMING - SIXTEENTH NOTES - COUNTED AS 1E &D 2 E & D 3 E & D 4 E & D

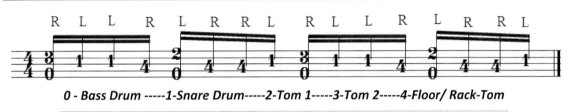

0 - Bass Drum -----1-Snare Drum-----2-Tom 1-----3-Tom 2-----4-Floor/ Rack-Tom

FOR THIS RUDIMENT TO WORK AS A BEAT, MAINTAIN THE TIMINGS AS WRITTEN. ONCE COMFORTABLE, MOVE THE LEFT HAND SINGLE STROKE PATTERN ACROSS THE HAND NUMBERS. DO THE SAME FOR THE RIGHT HAND. MAINTAIN ACCENT AS USUAL.

Day 6- Pattern - **R** L L **R L** R R **L**

Split Drum Numbers Tempo = 54 (+8)

TIMING - SIXTEENTH NOTES - COUNTED AS 1E &D 2 E & D 3 E & D 4 E & D

GUIDE

Similar to yesterday's, the left hand single part will be moved across the drum numbers in the table.

ACCENTS ARE ON 1 + AND OF 2 + 3 + AND OF 4

Hand Drum Numbers			
123	234	341	412
124	231	342	413
132	213	312	421
134	214	314	423
142	241	321	431
143	243	324	432

Day 7- Pattern - **R** L L **R L** R R **L**

Split Hand Drum Numbers Tempo = 54 (+8)

TIMING - SIXTEENTH NOTES - COUNTED AS 1E &D 2 E & D 3 E & D 4 E & D

GUIDE

Similar to yesterday's, the left hand single part will be moved across the drum numbers as shown in the table which includes the Hi-hat.

ACCENTS ARE ON **1** + AND OF **2** + **3** + AND OF **4**

BASS DRUM ON QUARTER NOTES.

Hand Drum Numbers			
12X	2X 4	X 41	412
124	2X 1	X 42	41X
1X 2	21X	X 12	421
1X 4	214	X 14	42X
142	241	X 21	4X 1
14X	24X	X 24	4X 2

Objective - Invert Paradiddle 2- Left Lead

The usual paradiddle pattern is **R** L R R **L** R L L. The second inverted Paradiddle we will be exploring is L L R **L** R R L **R**. This is another unique approach to improving our stick control and our Feet work. Apply on the drums to create different fills and a beat.   We will learn it in eighth note timings and finish off with sixteenth note timing (see below).

CONSIDER THE DYNAMIC LEVELS AS 6 FOR THE ACCENT AND 3 FOR THE UNACCENTED, WITH NO OTHER CHANGE IN VOLUME.

Beat of the Week

The drum beat will support all exercises this week. Always use a metronome at the set tempo. Keep an eye on both hands and feet while practicing to develop better technique and effective posture.

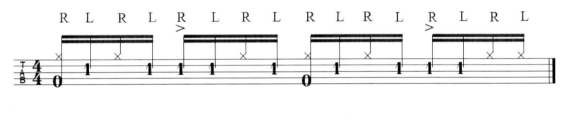

0 - Bass Drum　　　*1-Snare Drum*　　　*X- Hi Hat*

Day 1- Pattern - L L R **L** R R L **R**

Eighth Note Hand Tempo = 54 (+8)

TIMING - EIGHTH NOTES - COUNTED AS 1 & 2 & 3 & 4 &

GUIDE

Eighth Note Count Applied							
1	And	2	**And**	3	And	4	**And**
L	L	R	**L**	R	R	L	**R**

ACCENTS ARE ON AND OF 2 + AND OF 4

Day 2- Pattern - L L R **L** R R L **R**

Eighth Note Feet Tempo = 54 (+6)

<u>TIMING - EIGHTH NOTES - COUNTED AS **1 & 2 & 3 & 4 &**</u>

<u>GUIDE</u>

Eighth Note Count Applied							
1	And	2	**And**	3	And	4	**And**
L	L	R	**L**	R	R	L	**R**

<u>ACCENTS ARE ON AND **OF 2** + AND **OF 4**</u>

Day 3- Pattern - L L R **L** R R L **R**

Hand D.Numbers Tempo = 54 (+8)

TIMING - EIGHTH NOTES - COUNTED AS 1 & 2 & 3 & 4 &

GUIDE

Hand application, an example from the table - 3 1 2 4

Beat 1 + & gets drum 3 (LL), Beat 2 + & gets drum 1 (R**L**),
Beat 3 + & gets drum 2(RR), Beat 4 + & gets Drum 4 (L**R**)

ACCENTS ARE ON AND OF 2 + AND OF 4

BASS DRUM SHOULD HAVE STEADY QUARTER NOTE PULSE.

Drum Numbers			
1234	2341	3412	4123
1243	2314	3421	4132
1324	2134	3124	4213
1342	2143	3142	4231
1423	2413	3214	4312
1432	2431	3241	4321

Day 4- Pattern - L L R **L** R R L **R**

Sixteenth Note Hand Tempo = 54 (+8)

TIMING - SIXTEENTH NOTES - COUNTED AS 1E &D 2 E & D 3 E & D 4 E & D

GUIDE

Sixteenth Note Count Applied															
1	E	&	**D**	2	E	&	**D**	3	E	&	**D**	4	E	&	**D**
L	L	R	**L**	R	R	L	**R**	L	L	R	**L**	R	R	L	**R**

ACCENTS ARE ON THE **D** OF EACH QUARTER NOTE

Day 5 - Pattern - L L R **L** R R L **R**

Sixteenth Note Feet Tempo = 34 (+6)

<u>TIMING - SIXTEENTH NOTES - COUNTED AS 1E &D 2 E & D 3 E & D 4 E & D</u>

<u>GUIDE</u>

<u>ACCENTS ARE ON THE **D** OF EACH QUARTER NOTE</u>

Day 6- Pattern - L L R **L** R R L **R**

Hand + Feet D.Numbers Tempo = 54 (+8)

<u>TIMING - SIXTEENTH NOTES - COUNTED AS</u> 1E &D 2 E & D 3 E & D 4 E & D

<u>GUIDE</u>

Hand application, an example from the table - 3 1 2 4

Beat 1 gets drum 3 (LLR**L**), Beat 2gets drum 1 (RRL**R**),
Beat 3 gets drum 2(LLR**L**), Beat 4 gets Drum 4 (RRL**R**)

<u>ACCENTS ARE ON THE **D** OF EACH QUARTER NOTE</u>

BASS DRUM SHOULD HAVE STEADY QUARTER NOTE PULSE.

Hand Drum Numbers			
1234	2341	3412	4123
1243	2314	3421	4132
1324	2134	3124	4213
1342	2143	3142	4231
1423	2413	3214	4312
1432	2431	3241	4321

Day 7 - Pattern - L L R **L** R R L **R**

Split Hand + Feet D. Numbers Tempo = 54 (+8)

TIMING - SIXTEENTH NOTES - COUNTED AS 1E &D 2 E & D 3 E & D 4 E & D

GUIDE

Today's task is to split the limb.

- Play the Left hand with the Right leg (**HHLHLLHL**)
- Play the Left leg with the Right hand (**LLHLHHLH**)

Hand Drum Numbers			
1234	2341	3412	4123
1243	2314	3421	4132
1324	2134	3124	4213
1342	2143	3142	4231
1423	2413	3214	4312
1432	2431	3241	4321

Objective - Drag - Right Lead

The drag rudiment in some circles is known as the ruff. A drag incorporates the use of ghost notes which are silent musical parts before the main accented part.   The ghosted note is a double on one limb before an accented single on the other. For our right limb lead, the pattern is $_{LL}$R $_{RR}$L. The drag is a rudiment based on quarter note timing with the accented parts highlighting the 1 2 3 4 of the quarter note count. However for learning, we will spread it across 16th notes count.

CONSIDER THE DYNAMIC LEVELS AS 6 FOR THE ACCENT AND 3 FOR THE UNACCENTED, WITH NO OTHER CHANGE IN VOLUME.

Beat of the Week

The drum beat will support all exercises this week. Always use a metronome at the set tempo. Keep an eye on both hands and feet while practicing to develop better technique and effective posture.

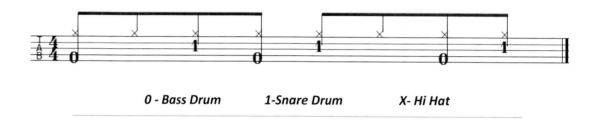

0 - Bass Drum   *1-Snare Drum*   *X- Hi Hat*

Day 1- Pattern - LL **R** RR**L**

Sixteenth Note Hand Tempo = 54 (+8)

TIMING - QUARTER NOTES - COUNTED AS 1 2 3 4

GUIDE

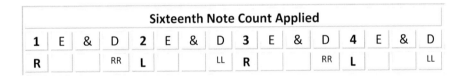

Sixteenth Note Count Applied															
1	E	&	D	**2**	E	&	D	**3**	E	&	D	**4**	E	&	D
R		RR	**L**			LL	**R**			RR	**L**			LL

ACCENTS ARE ON EACH QUARTER NOTE 1 2 3 4 .

Day 2 - Pattern - LL **R** RR**L**

Sixteenth Note Feet Tempo = 30 (+6)

TIMING - QUARTER NOTES - COUNTED AS **1 2 3 4**

GUIDE

Sixteenth Note Count Applied															
1	E	&	D	**2**	E	&	D	**3**	E	&	D	**4**	E	&	D
R			RR	L			LL	R			RR	L			LL

ACCENTS ARE ON EACH QUARTER NOTE **1 2 3 4** .

Day 3- Pattern - LL **R** RR**L**

Split Hand D.Numbers Tempo = 54 (+8)

TIMING - QUARTER NOTES - COUNTED AS 1 2 3 4

GUIDE

Hand application, an example from the table - 3 4

Left hand remains on the first number **(3)**, whilst Right hand remains on the second number **(4)**.

ACCENTS ARE ON EACH QUARTER NOTE 1 2 3 4 .

BASS DRUM SHOULD HAVE STEADY QUARTER NOTE PULSE.

Drum Numbers			
12	23	32	41
13	24	34	42
14	21	31	43
1X	2X	3X	4X

Day 4 - Pattern - LL **R** RR**L**

Split Hand and Foot D. Numbers Tempo = 54 (+8)

TIMING - QUARTER NOTES - COUNTED AS **1 2 3 4**

GUIDE

Hand application, an example from the table

Left Hand - Y 1

The first number / letter will be playing the silent doubles (LL), whilst
the second number / letter will be playing the accented single **(R)**
with the left hand.

Drum Numbers			
Left Hand		Right Hand	
01	10	10	01
02	20	20	02
03	30	30	03
04	40	40	04
0X	X0	X0	0X
Y1	1Y	1Y	Y1
Y2	2Y	2Y	Y2
Y3	3Y	3Y	Y3
Y4	4Y	4Y	Y4
YX	XY	XY	YX

136

Day 5 - Pattern - LL **R** RR**L**

Pattern as a Beat Tempo = 54 (+8)

<u>TIMING - QUARTER NOTES - COUNTED AS **1 2 3 4**</u>

<u>GUIDE</u>

0 - Bass Drum   *1-Snare Drum*   *X- Hi-Hat*

Accent is on each Quarter note

Day 6 - Pattern - LL **R** RR**L**

Full Hand Pattern Applied to Drum Numbers Tempo = 54 (+8)

TIMING - QUARTER NOTES - COUNTED AS **1 2 3 4**

GUIDE

Hand application, an example from the table - 3 4 1 2

Drum 3 (LL**R** RR**L)**, Drum 4 (LL**R** RR**L)**,
Drum 1 (LL**R** RR**L)**, Drum 2 (LL**R** RR**L)**

THIS IS A TWO BAR PATTERN.

Hand Drum Numbers			
1234	2341	3412	4123
1243	2314	3421	4132
1324	2134	3124	4213
1342	2143	3142	4231
1423	2413	3214	4312
1432	2431	3241	4321

Day 7 - Pattern - LL **R** RR**L**

Full Hand Pattern Applied to D.N With Bass Drum Tempo = 54 (+8)

TIMING - QUARTER NOTES - COUNTED AS **1 2 3 4**

GUIDE

Similar to yesterday's exercise with the bass drum playing the 'AND' of each quarter note.

This is a two bar pattern with the bass drum on the 'And' of each quarter note.

Hand Drum Numbers			
1234	2341	3412	4123
1243	2314	3421	4132
1324	2134	3124	4213
1342	2143	3142	4231
1423	2413	3214	4312
1432	2431	3241	4321

Objective - Pataflafla - Right Lead

When I first heard it, I thought it was a joke but Pataflafla is an actual rudiment; an interesting one as well. Pataflafla is a four-note pattern with flams on the first and last note. Out of a total of 16 notes to be played in the form of a single stroke roll, 8 of the notes are actually flams on the da of the 16th notes count and the quarter notes. We will be learning it in eighth notes. You can consider it as the first note is a flam and the last note is a flam for every quarter note value. Below is the original sixteenth note version.

<u>CONSIDER THE DYNAMIC LEVELS AS **6** FOR THE ACCENT AND **3** FOR THE UNACCENTED, WITH NO OTHER CHANGE IN VOLUME.</u>

The pattern broken down is ᵣ**R** L R ᵣ**L** .

Beat of the Week

The drum beat will support all exercises this week. Always use a metronome at the set tempo. Keep an eye on both hands and feet while practicing to develop better technique and effective posture.

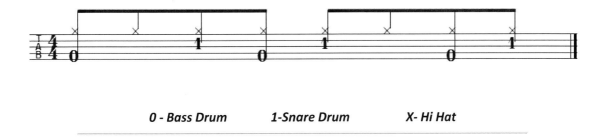

0 - Bass Drum   *1-Snare Drum*   *X- Hi Hat*

Day 1- Pattern - L**R** L R R**L** **R** L R R**L**

Eighth Note Hand Tempo = 54 (+8)

TIMING - EIGHTH NOTES - COUNTED AS 1 & 2 & 3 & 4 &

GUIDE

Eighth Note Count Applied										
d	**1**	And	2	e	**And**	**3**	And	4	e	**And**
l	**R**	L	R	r	**L**	**R**	L	R	r	**L**

ACCENTS ARE IN BOLD

Day 2- Pattern - L**R** L R R**L R** L R R**L**

Eighth Note Feet Tempo = 34 (+8)

TIMING - EIGHTH NOTES - COUNTED AS 1 & 2 & 3 & 4 &

GUIDE

Eighth Note Count Applied										
d	**1**	And	2	e	**And**	**3**	And	4	e	**And**
l	**R**	L	R	r	**L**	**R**	L	R	r	**L**

ACCENTS ARE IN BOLD

Day 3- Pattern - L**R** L R R**L** **R** L R R**L**

Full Hand Pattern Applied to Drum Numbers Tempo = 54 (+8)

<u>TIMING - EIGHTH NOTES - COUNTED AS **1 & 2 & 3 & 4 &**</u>

<u>GUIDE</u>

Hand application, an example from the table - 3 4 1 2

Drum 3 (L**R** L R R**L** **R** L R R**L**), Drum 4 (L**R** L R R**L** **R** L R R**L**), Drum 1 (L**R** L R R**L** **R** L R R**L**), Drum 2 (L**R** L R R**L** **R** L R R**L**)

This is a 2 bar pattern.

Hand Drum Numbers			
1234	2341	3412	4123
1243	2314	3421	4132
1324	2134	3124	4213
1342	2143	3142	4231
1423	2413	3214	4312
1432	2431	3241	4321

Day 4 - Pattern - L**R** L R R**L** **R** L R R**L**

Hand Accents Applied to Drum Numbers Tempo = 54 (+8)

<u>TIMING - EIGHTH NOTES - COUNTED AS **1 & 2 & 3 & 4 &**</u>

<u>GUIDE</u>

The pattern L**R** L R R**L** **R** L R R**L** is played on the snare drum (1) or any drum including hi-hat. However, every accent to be played, should be played according to the drum numbers. There are four accents altogether.

<u>THIS IS A **1** BAR PATTERN</u>

Hand Drum Numbers			
1234	2341	3412	4123
1243	2314	3421	4132
1324	2134	3124	4213
1342	2143	3142	4231
1423	2413	3214	4312
1432	2431	3241	4321

145

Day 5 - Pattern - L**R** L R R**L** **R** L R R**L**

Split Hand D. Numbers Tempo = 54 (+8)

<u>TIMING - EIGHTH NOTES - COUNTED AS **1 & 2 & 3 & 4 &**</u>

<u>GUIDE</u>

Hand application, an example from the table - 3 4

Left hand remains on the first number **(3)**, whilst Right hand remains on the second number **(4)**.

<u>BASS DRUM SHOULD HAVE STEADY QUARTER NOTE PULSE.</u>

Drum Numbers			
12	23	32	41
13	24	34	42
14	21	31	43
1X	2X	3X	4X

Day 6 - Pattern - L**R** L R R**L** **R** L R R**L**

Split Hand Continued D. Numbers Tempo = 54 (+8)

<u>Timing - Eighth Notes - Counted as **1 & 2 & 3 & 4 &**</u>

<u>Guide</u>

Hand application, an example from the table - R 3

Left hand remains on the first number **(R - Ride Cymbal)**, whilst Right hand remains on the second number **(3)**.

Feel free to setup multiple ride cymbals or move your ride closer to your left hand or use your crash cymbal.

<u>**Bass drum should have steady quarter note pulse.**</u>

Drum Numbers	
R1	1R
R2	2R
R3	3R
R4	4R
RX	XR

Day 7- Pattern - L**R** L R R**L** **R** L R R**L**

Eighth Note Feet Tempo = 34 (+8)

TIMING - EIGHTH NOTES - COUNTED AS 1 & 2 & 3 & 4 &

GUIDE

Eighth Note Count Applied										
d	**1**	And	2	e	**And**	**3**	And	4	e	**And**
l	**R**	L	R	r	**L**	**R**	L	R	r	**L**

PLAY STEADY QUARTER NOTES ON THE RIGHT HAND, THEN SWAP TO LEFT HAND.

ACCENTS ARE IN BOLD

Objective-Freestyle Mix of Past Rudiments

Mix all the various exercises we have learnt into a variety of combinations as follows, using daily application method daily.

Day	Rudiments To Mix	Daily Application Method
1	Single Stroke + Double Stroke	Hands
2	5 Stroke Roll + Paradiddle	Feet
3	Single Stroke 4 + Inverted Double 1	Split Limbs
4	Single Stroke 7 + 10 Stroke Roll	Across Drum Numbers
5	Inverted Paradiddle + Drag	Accent Across Drum Numbers
6	Pataflafla + Inverted Double	Accent On Snare Drum
7	Inverted Paradiddle 2 + Single Stroke 7	Across Cymbals

Keep an eye on both hands and feet while practicing to develop better technique and posture.

Objective - Five Stroke Roll - Right Lead

We have already looked at this rudiment in week 4 from a left limb lead perspective. As you will recall, the five stroke roll engages 2 double strokes and 1 single stroke.

This week, we will be leading with the right limbs.

CONSIDER THE DYNAMIC LEVELS AS **6** FOR THE ACCENT AND **3** FOR THE UNACCENTED, WITH NO OTHER CHANGE IN VOLUME.

The pattern is by R R L L **R** followed L L R R **L**.

Beat of the Week

The drum beat will support all exercises this week. Always use a metronome at the set tempo. Keep an eye on both hands and feet while practicing to develop better technique and effective posture.

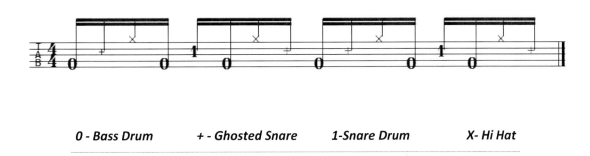

0 - Bass Drum   + - Ghosted Snare   1-Snare Drum   X- Hi Hat

Day 1- Pattern - R R L L **R** L L R R **L**

Six Eighth Note Hand Tempo = 54 (+8)

TIMING - SIX EIGHT NOTES - COUNTED AS 1 2 3 4 5 6

GUIDE

Six Eight Note Count Applied					
1	2	3	4	**5**	6
R	R	L	L	**R**	
L	L	R	R	**L**	

ACCENTS ARE IN BOLD

Day 2 - Pattern - R R L L **R** L L R R **L**

Six Eighth Note Feet Tempo = 54 (+8)

TIMING - SIX EIGHT NOTES - COUNTED AS 1 2 3 4 5 6

GUIDE

Six Eight Note Count Applied					
1	2	3	4	**5**	6
R	R	L	L	**R**	
L	L	R	R	**L**	

ACCENTS ARE IN BOLD

Day 3 - Pattern - R R L L **R** L L R R **L**

Hand Accents Applied to Drum Numbers Tempo = 54 (+8)

TIMING - SIX EIGHT NOTES - COUNTED AS 1 2 3 4 5 6

GUIDE

The pattern R R L L **R** L L R R **L** is played on the snare drum (1) or any drum including hi-hat. However, every accent to be played, should be played according to the drum numbers.

THIS IS A **4** BAR PATTERN

Hand Drum Numbers			
1234	2341	3412	4123
1243	2314	3421	4132
1324	2134	3124	4213
1342	2143	3142	4231
1423	2413	3214	4312
1432	2431	3241	4321

Day 4 - Pattern - R R L L **R** L L R R **L**

Hand Accents Applied to D.numbers and Cymbals Tempo = 54 (+8)
TIMING - SIX EIGHT NOTES - COUNTED AS 1 2 3 4 5 6

GUIDE

The pattern R R L L **R** on first number, L L R R **L on second number and so on** is played according to the drum numbers with accent on Cymbals.

Bass drum should have quarter notes on beats 1, 3 and 5.

Multiple cymbals will be ideal.

THIS IS A 4 BAR PATTERN

Hand Drum Numbers			
1234	2341	3412	4123
1243	2314	3421	4132
1324	2134	3124	4213
1342	2143	3142	4231
1423	2413	3214	4312
1432	2431	3241	4321

155

Day 5 - Pattern - R R L L **R** L L R R **L**

Hand Pattern with Bass to Drum Numbers Tempo = 54 (+8)

<u>TIMING - SIX EIGHT NOTES - COUNTED AS **1** 2 3 4 5 **6**</u>

<u>GUIDE</u>

The pattern R R L L **R** L L R R **L** is played on the snare drum (1)
However, every accent to be played, should be played according to
the drum numbers. The Bass drum is added just on beat 6 at the
end of the pattern.

Bass drum is on beat 6 of each bar.

<u>THIS IS A **4** BAR PATTERN</u>

156

Hand Drum Numbers			
1234	2341	3412	4123
1243	2314	3421	4132
1324	2134	3124	4213
1342	2143	3142	4231
1423	2413	3214	4312
1432	2431	3241	4321

Day 6 - Pattern - R R L L **R** L L R R **L**

Sixteenth Note Hand Tempo = 54 (+8)

TIMING - SIXTEENTH NOTES - COUNTED AS 1E &D 2 E & D 3 E & D 4 E & D

GUIDE

ONCE ACHIEVED, APPLY TO DRUM NUMBERS WITH ALL FIVE STROKES ON 1 DRUM SURFACE, OR EXPERIMENT
AROUND THE KIT USING THE DRUM NUMBERS.

Day 7 - Pattern - R R L L **R** L L R R **L**

Hand Pattern with Bass Drum Tempo = 54 (+8)

TIMING - SIXTEENTH NOTES - COUNTED AS 1E &D 2 E & D 3 E & D 4 E & D

GUIDE

Sixteenth Note Count Applied															
1	E	&	D	**2**	E	&	D	3	E	&	D	**4**	E	&	D
R	R	L	L	**R**	0		L	L	R	R	**L**	0			

SIMILAR TO YESTERDAY'S, **5** STROKES PER DRUM SURFACE. HOWEVER, BASS DRUM SHOULD BE INCLUDED ON THE AND OF 2 + THE AND OF 4 AS SHOWN ABOVE.

Objective - Single Ratamacue - Right Lead

Ratamacue is similar to single stroke 4, which is based on a 16th note triplet count. The differences are the double ghost notes before the first main note and the accent is on the last note. Ratamacue is an alternating rudiment.

To achieve the most realistic sound, it is best to play it pronounced as, "A Ra ta ma cue". The 'A' taking the place of the two ghost notes, whilst Ra (R) ta (L) Ma (R) Cue (**L**).

<u>CONSIDER THE DYNAMIC LEVELS AS **6** FOR THE ACCENT AND **3** FOR THE UNACCENTED, WITH NO OTHER CHANGE IN VOLUME.</u>

As a pattern, it looks like this _{LL}R L R **L** _{RR}L R L **R**.

Beat of the Week

The drum beat will support all exercises this week. Always use a metronome at the set tempo. Keep an eye on both hands and feet while practicing to develop better technique and effective posture.

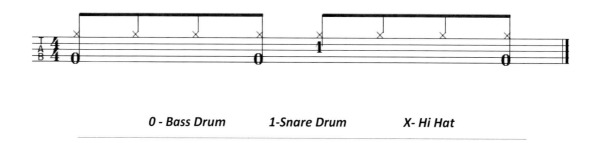

0 - Bass Drum   **1-Snare Drum**   **X- Hi Hat**

Day 1- Pattern - LLR L R **L** RRL R L **R**

Eighth Note Triplet Hand Tempo = 54 (+8)

TIMING - EIGHTH NOTES TRIPLET - COUNTED AS 1 TRIP LET 2 TRIP LET 3 TRIP LET 4 TRIP LET

GUIDE

	1	Trip	Let	2	Trip	Let		3	Trip	Let	4	Trip	Let
LL	R	L	R	**L**			RR	L	R	L	**R**		

ACCENTS ARE IN BOLD

Day 2 - Pattern - LLR L R **L** RRL R L **R**

Eighth Note Triplet Feet Tempo = 30 (+8)

TIMING - EIGHTH NOTES TRIPLET - COUNTED AS 1 TRIP LET 2 TRIP LET 3 TRIP LET 4 TRIP LET

GUIDE

		1	Trip	Let	2	Trip	Let	3	Trip	Let	4	Trip	Let

	1	Trip	Let	2	Trip	Let		3	Trip	Let	4	Trip	Let
LL	R	L	R	**L**			RR	L	R	L	**R**		

ACCENTS ARE IN BOLD

Day 3 - Pattern - LLR L R **L** RRL R L **R**

Hand Accents Applied to Drum Numbers Tempo = 54 (+8)

TIMING - EIGHTH NOTES TRIPLET - COUNTED AS 1 TRIP LET 2 TRIP LET 3 TRIP LET 4 TRIP LET

GUIDE

The pattern LLR L R **L** RRL R L **R** is played on the snare drum (1) or any drum including hi-hat. However, every accent to be played, should be played according to the drum numbers.

THIS IS A **2** BAR PATTERN

Hand Drum Numbers			
1234	2341	3412	4123
1243	2314	3421	4132
1324	2134	3124	4213
1342	2143	3142	4231
1423	2413	3214	4312
1432	2431	3241	4321

Day 4 - Pattern - LLR L R **L** RRL R L **R**

Split Hand D.Numbers Tempo = 54 (+8)

TIMING - EIGHTH NOTES TRIPLET - COUNTED AS 1 TRIP LET 2 TRIP LET 3 TRIP LET 4 TRIP LET

GUIDE

Hand application, an example from the table - 3 4

Left hand remains on the first number **(3)**, whilst Right hand remains on the second number **(4)**.

BASS DRUM SHOULD HAVE STEADY QUARTER NOTE PULSE.

Drum Numbers			
12	23	32	41
13	24	34	42
14	21	31	43
1X	2X	3X	4X

Day 5 - Pattern - LLR L R **L** RRL R L **R**

Split Hand + Foot D.Numbers Tempo = 54 (+8)

TIMING - EIGHTH NOTES TRIPLET - COUNTED AS 1 TRIP LET 2 TRIP LET 3 TRIP LET 4 TRIP LET

GUIDE

Application,

Y = Left Leg / Hi- Hat foot

The first number / letter will be playing represents the (L) part of the rudiment,   whilst the second number / letter will be playing the (R) part with indicated limb.

Drum Numbers			
Left Hand		**Right Hand**	
01	10	10	01
02	20	20	02
03	30	30	03
04	40	40	04
0X	X0	X0	0X
Y1	1Y	1Y	Y1
Y2	2Y	2Y	Y2
Y3	3Y	3Y	Y3
Y4	4Y	4Y	Y4
YX	XY	XY	YX

Day 6 - Pattern - LLR L R **L** RRL R L **R**

Pattern as a Beat Tempo = 54 (+8)

GUIDE

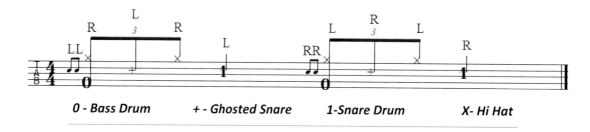

0 - Bass Drum   *+ - Ghosted Snare*   *1-Snare Drum*   *X- Hi Hat*

ACCENT IS ON BEAT **2** AND **4**

Day 7 - Pattern - LLR L R **L** RRL R L **R**

Eighth Note Triplet Hand and Feet Tempo = 44 (+8)

TIMING - EIGHTH NOTES TRIPLET - COUNTED AS 1 TRIP LET 2 TRIP LET 3 TRIP LET 4 TRIP LET

GUIDE

	Eighth Note triplet Count											
	1	Trip	Let	**2**	Trip	Let	3	Trip	Let	**4**	Trip	Let
LL	R	L	R	**L**			RR	L	R	L	**R**		

THE RUDIMENT SHOULD BE PLAYED ON THE FEET WHILST THE HAND SWITCHES BETWEEN QUARTER NOTES AND EIGHTH NOTES.

Objective - Flam Drag - Right Lead

Though we have not actually learnt the flam, a flam drag is interesting to play as it is based on triplets.   Flam drag is in the flam rudiment group that consists of a single grace note followed by an eighth note triplet with two sixteenth note strokes on the second third of the triplet then finishing with a single. The sticking pattern shown below is the accepted method of performing a flam drag. This is an alternating rudiment.

<u>**CONSIDER THE DYNAMIC LEVELS AS 6 FOR THE ACCENT AND 3 FOR THE UNACCENTED, WITH NO OTHER CHANGE IN VOLUME.**</u>

The pattern is I**R** L L R r**L** R R L

Beat of the Week

The drum beat will support all exercises this week. Always use a metronome at the set tempo. Keep an eye on both hands and feet while practicing to develop better technique and effective posture.

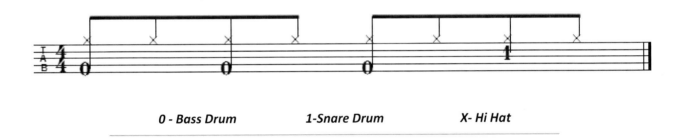

0 - Bass Drum　　　*1-Snare Drum*　　　*X- Hi Hat*

Day 1-Pattern - l**R** LL R - r**L** RR L

Eighth Note Triplet Hand Tempo = 54 (+8)

TIMING - EIGHTH NOTE TRIPLET - COUNTED AS 1 TRIP LET 2 TRIP LET 3 TRIP LET 4 TRIP LET

GUIDE

Eighth Note triplet Count											
1	Trip	Let	**2**	Trip	Let	**3**	Trip	Let	**4**	Trip	Let
l**R**	LL	R	r**L**	RR	L	l**R**	LL	R	r**L**	RR	L

ACCENT IS ON EACH QUARTER NOTE.

Day 2 - Pattern - l**R** LL R - r**L** RR L

Eighth Note Triplet Feet Tempo = 44 (+8)

TIMING - EIGHTH NOTE TRIPLET - COUNTED AS 1 TRIP LET 2 TRIP LET 3 TRIP LET 4 TRIP LET

<u>GUIDE</u>

Eighth Note triplet Count											
1	Trip	Let	**2**	Trip	Let	**3**	Trip	Let	**4**	Trip	Let
l**R**	LL	R	r**L**	RR	L	l**R**	LL	R	r**L**	RR	L

<u>ACCENT IS ON EACH QUARTER NOTE.</u>

Day 3 - Pattern - lR LL R - rL RR L

Hi-Hat Hand Tempo = 54 (+8)

TIMING - EIGHTH NOTE TRIPLET - COUNTED AS 1 TRIP LET 2 TRIP LET 3 TRIP LET 4 TRIP LET

GUIDE

Play the Flam Drag pattern on the Hi-hat firmly closed, whilst playing steady quarter notes on the bass drum. Start slowly making sure the accents are correctly placed.

Accent is on each quarter note, 1 2 3 4.

Day 4 - Pattern - l**R** LL R - r**L** RR L

Half Hand Pattern Applied to Drum Numbers Tempo = 54 (+8)

TIMING - EIGHTH NOTE TRIPLET - COUNTED AS 1 TRIP LET 2 TRIP LET 3 TRIP LET 4 TRIP LET

GUIDE

Hand application, an example from the table - 3 4 1 2

    Drum 3 (l**R**LLR), Drum 4 (r**L**RRL), Drum 1 (l**R**LLR), Drum 2 (r**L**RRL)

Add the bass drum on each quarter note.

THIS IS A **1** BAR PATTERN

Hand Drum Numbers			
1234	2341	3412	4123
1243	2314	3421	4132
1324	2134	3124	4213
1342	2143	3142	4231
1423	2413	3214	4312
1432	2431	3241	4321

173

Day 5 - Pattern - l**R** LL R - r**L** RR L

Split Hand + Feet Drum Numbers Tempo = 54 (+8)

TIMING - EIGHTH NOTE TRIPLET - COUNTED AS 1 TRIP LET 2 TRIP LET 3 TRIP LET 4 TRIP LET

<u>GUIDE</u>

Application,

The first number / letter will be playing represents the R part of the rudiment, whilst the second number / letter will be playing represents the L part of the rudiment.

Drum Numbers			
Split Limbs		**Abbreviation Guide**	
O	LH	0	Bass Drum
RH	O	RH	Right Hand
Y	RH	Y	Left Foot
LH	Y	LH	Left Hand
O	RH		
RH	Y		
Y	LH		
LH	O		

Day 6 - Pattern - lR LL R - rL RR L

Cymbal Tempo = 54 (+8)

TIMING - EIGHTH NOTE TRIPLET - COUNTED AS 1 TRIP LET 2 TRIP LET 3 TRIP LET 4 TRIP LET

HAND GUIDE

Play the flam drag pattern on one crash cymbal or multiple cymbals,   maintaining accents on beats 1 2 3 4.

The pattern can be played as normal for multiple bars to build ambience in a ballad song or at the end.

Try the pattern with and without the bass drum for a variation of effects.

Day 7 - Pattern - lR LL R - rL RR L

Hand Accents Applied to Drum Numbers Tempo = 54 (+8)
TIMING - EIGHTH NOTE TRIPLET - COUNTED AS 1 TRIP LET 2 TRIP LET 3 TRIP LET 4 TRIP LET

GUIDE

The flam drag pattern is played on the hi-hat or any drum of choice including snare drum. However, every accent to be played, should be played according to the drum numbers.

PLAY NOTES AS CLOSE TOGETHER AS POSSIBLE, BASS DRUM PLAYING ALL QUARTER NOTES.

Hand Drum Numbers			
1234	2341	3412	4123
1243	2314	3421	4132
1324	2134	3124	4213
1342	2143	3142	4231
1423	2413	3214	4312
1432	2431	3241	4321

Objective - Flam - Right Lead

Flam is a tap stroke that gives you a larger sound from your sticks. The effect of adding power and warmth to the basic stroke is created when a flam is used. Think of the dynamic levels of a flam as follows: The first / the quietest note is a 1 on the scale and the second / accented note is a 6.

CONSIDER THE DYNAMIC LEVELS AS **6** FOR THE ACCENT AND **1** FOR THE UNACCENTED, WITH NO OTHER CHANGE IN VOLUME.

The pattern is ₗ**R** ᵣ **L** (Right Lead) or ᵣ**L** ₗ**R** (Left Lead).

Beat of the Week

The drum beat will support all exercises this week. Always use a metronome at the set tempo. Keep an eye on both hands and feet while practicing to develop better technique and effective posture.

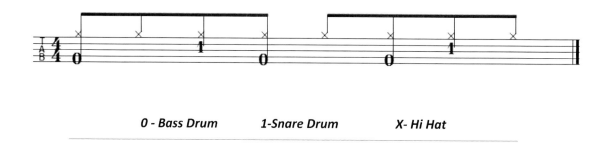

0 - Bass Drum   **1-Snare Drum**   **X- Hi Hat**

Day 1- Pattern - L**R** R**L** L**R** R**L**

Quarter Note Hand Tempo = 54 (+8)

TIMING - QUARTER NOTES - COUNTED AS **1 2 3 4**

GUIDE

Quarter Note count Applied			
1	2	3	4
LR	RL	LR	RL

PLAY NOTES AS CLOSE TOGETHER AS POSSIBLE, MAINTAINING THE HAND SWAP.

Day 2 - Pattern - L**R** **R**L L**R** **R**L

Quarter Note Feet Tempo = 54 (+8)

TIMING - QUARTER NOTES - COUNTED AS 1 2 3 4

GUIDE

Quarter Note count Applied			
1	2	3	4
L**R**	**R**L	L**R**	**R**L

Day 3 - Pattern - L**R** R**L** L**R** R**L**

Hand Applied to Drum Numbers Tempo = 54 (+8)

TIMING - QUARTER NOTES - COUNTED AS 1 2 3 4

GUIDE

Hand application, an example from the table - 3 4 1 2

Drum 3 (L**R**), Drum 4 (R**L**), Drum 1 (L**R**), Drum 2 (R**L**)

Add the bass drum on each quarter note.

THIS IS A **1** BAR PATTERN

Hand Drum Numbers			
1234	2341	3412	4123
1243	2314	3421	4132
1324	2134	3124	4213
1342	2143	3142	4231
1423	2413	3214	4312
1432	2431	3241	4321

Day 4 - Pattern - LR RL LR RL

Split Hand D.Numbers Tempo = 54 (+8)

<u>TIMING - QUARTER NOTES - COUNTED AS **1 2 3 4**</u>

<u>GUIDE</u>

Hand application, an example from the table - 3 4

Left hand remains on the first number **(3)**, whilst Right hand remains on the second number **(4)**.

<u>**BASS DRUM SHOULD HAVE STEADY QUARTER NOTE PULSE.**</u>

Drum Numbers			
12	23	32	41
13	24	34	42
14	21	31	43
1X	2X	3X	4X

Day 5 - Pattern - L**R** R**L** L**R** R**L**

Split Hand + Foot D.Numbers Tempo = 54 (+8)

TIMING - QUARTER NOTES - COUNTED AS 1 2 3 4

GUIDE

Application,

Y = Left Leg / Hi- Hat foot

The first number / letter will be playing represents the L part of
the rudiment, whilst the second number / letter will be playing
represents the R part of the rudiment.

Drum Numbers			
Left Hand		Right Hand	
01	10	10	01
02	20	20	02
03	30	30	03
04	40	40	04
0X	X0	X0	0X
Y1	1Y	1Y	Y1
Y2	2Y	2Y	Y2
Y3	3Y	3Y	Y3
Y4	4Y	4Y	Y4
YX	XY	XY	YX

Day 6 - Pattern - L**R** R**L** L**R** R**L**

Hi-Hat Hand Tempo = 54 (+8)

<u>TIMING - QUARTER NOTES - COUNTED AS 1 2 3 4</u>

<u>GUIDE</u>

Play the flam pattern on the hi-hat firmly closed, whilst playing steady quarter notes on the bass drum. Start slowly making sure the accents are correctly placed.

Accent is on each quarter note count, 1 2 3 4.

Day 7 - Pattern - L**R** R**L** L**R** R**L**

Cymbal Tempo = 54 (+8)

TIMING - QUARTER NOTES - COUNTED AS 1 2 3 4

GUIDE

Play the flam pattern on the one crash cymbal or multiple cymbals at the end of a fill, crashing on beat 1.

The pattern can be played as normal for multiple bars to build ambience in a ballad song.

Try the pattern with and without the bass drum for a variation of effects.

Objective - Multiple Bounce Roll - Left Lead

Multiple bounce roll is simply letting the stick bounce till it comes to a complete stop naturally then swapping limbs around. However, you want to achieve a complete cycle (beginning to end) within a specific time period such as a quarter note before starting the next cycle on the opposite limb. This rudiment is better achieved by the hands, therefore we will try it out on the hands but still give it a go on the feet. This rudiment is also known as the buzz roll, press roll, military roll and the standard 'Drum roll please'. <u>CONSIDER THE DYNAMIC LEVELS AS **3**, WITH NO CHANGE IN VOLUME.</u>

Written as

Played As

Beat of the Week

The drum beat will support all exercises this week. Always use a metronome at the set tempo. Keep an eye on both hands and feet while practicing to develop better technique and effective posture.

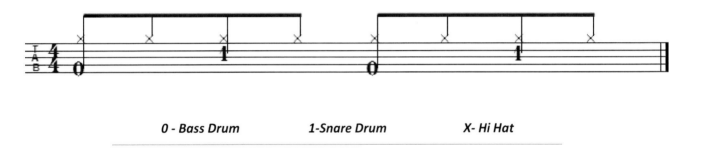

0 - Bass Drum　　　*1-Snare Drum*　　　*X- Hi Hat*

Day 1-Pattern - ~~L~~ ~~R~~

Quarter Note Hand Tempo = 5̶4̶ (+8)

TIMING - QUARTER NOTES - COUNTED AS 1 2 3 4

GUIDE

Quarter Note Count Applied			
1	2	3	4
~~L~~	~~R~~	~~L~~	~~R~~

This exercise should be applied on just a single surface. This can be either a practice pad or snare drum.

REMEMBER, THERE IS NO CHANGE IN VOLUME.

Day 2-Pattern - ~~L~~ ~~R~~

Quarter Note Feet Tempo = 54 (+8)

TIMING - QUARTER NOTES - COUNTED AS 1 2 3 4

GUIDE

Quarter Note Count Applied			
1	2	3	4
~~L~~	~~R~~	~~L~~	~~R~~

This exercise should be applied on just a single surface. This can be either a practice pad or snare drum.

REMEMBER, THERE IS NO CHANGE IN VOLUME.

Day 3 -Pattern - ~~L~~ R̶

Full Hand Pattern Applied to Drum Numbers Tempo = 54 (+8)

TIMING - QUARTER NOTES - COUNTED AS 1 2 3 4

GUIDE

Hand application, an example from the table - 3 4 1 2

Drum 3 (L̶), Drum 4 (R̶), Drum 1 (L̶), Drum 2(R̶)

THIS IS A 1 BAR PATTERN

Hand Drum Numbers			
1234	2341	3412	4123
1243	2314	3421	4132
1324	2134	3124	4213
1342	2143	3142	4231
1423	2413	3214	4312
1432	2431	3241	4321

Day 4 -Pattern - ~~L~~ ~~R~~

Eighth Note Hand Tempo = 54 (+8)

TIMING - EIGHTH NOTES - COUNTED AS 1 & 2 & 3 & 4 &

GUIDE

Eighth Note Count Applied							
1	And	2	And	3	And	4	And
~~L~~	~~R~~	~~L~~	~~R~~	~~L~~	~~R~~	~~L~~	~~R~~

Maintain equal volume throughout especially on Beat 1. Maintain equal volume throughout especially on Beat 1.

Day 5 -Pattern - ~~L~~ ~~R~~

Eighth Note Feet Tempo = 44 (+8)

TIMING - EIGHTH NOTES - COUNTED AS 1 & 2 & 3 & 4 &

GUIDE

Eighth Note Count Applied							
1	And	2	And	3	And	4	And
~~L~~	~~R~~	~~L~~	~~R~~	~~L~~	~~R~~	~~L~~	~~R~~

Maintain equal volume throughout especially on Beat 1. Maintain equal volume throughout especially on Beat 1.

Day 6 -Pattern - ~~L~~ ~~R~~

Full Hand Pattern Applied to Drum Numbers Tempo = 54 (+8)

TIMING - EIGHTH NOTES - COUNTED AS 1 & 2 & 3 & 4 &

GUIDE

Hand application, an example from the table - 3 4   1 2

  Drum 3 (~~L~~~~R~~), Drum 4 (~~L~~~~R~~), Drum 1 (~~L~~~~R~~), Drum 2(~~L~~~~R~~)

THIS IS A 1 BAR PATTERN

Hand Drum Numbers			
1234	2341	3412	4123
1243	2314	3421	4132
1324	2134	3124	4213
1342	2143	3142	4231
1423	2413	3214	4312
1432	2431	3241	4321

Day 7 - Pattern - ~~L~~ ~~R~~

Split Hand+Foot Drum Numbers Tempo = 54 (+8)

TIMING - EIGHTH NOTES - COUNTED AS 1 & 2 & 3 & 4 &

GUIDE

Application,

The first number / letter will be playing represents the L part of the rudiment, whilst the second number / letter will be playing represents the R part of the rudiment.

EXAMPLE LH - Y

LH (L) Y (R)

Drum Numbers			
Split Limbs		Abbreviation Guide	
O	LH	0	Bass Drum
RH	O	RH	Right Hand
Y	RH	Y	Left Foot
LH	Y	LH	Left Foot
O	RH		
RH	Y		
Y	LH		
LH	O		

Objective - Flam Accent - Right Hand Lead

Flam accent is simply an alternating triplet pattern with the quarter notes being flams (with accents). The timing for this is usually eighth note triplets.

<u>CONSIDER THE DYNAMIC LEVELS AS **6** FOR THE ACCENT AND **3** FOR THE UNACCENTED, WITH NO OTHER CHANGE IN VOLUME.</u>

The right hand pattern for a flam accent is ₗR L R ᵣL R L .

Beat of the Week

The drum beat will support all exercises this week. Always use a metronome at the set tempo. Keep an eye on both hands and feet while practicing to develop better technique and effective posture.

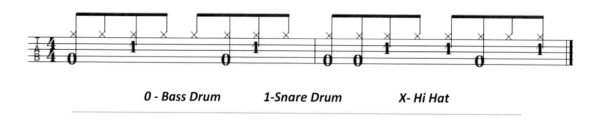

0 - Bass Drum   *1-Snare Drum*   *X- Hi Hat*

Day 1- Pattern - L**R** L R R**L** R L

Six Eighth Note Hand Tempo = 54 (+8)

<u>TIMING - SIX EIGHT NOTES - COUNTED AS 1 2 3 4 5 6</u>

<u>GUIDE</u>

Six Eight Note Count Applied					
1	2	3	**4**	5	6
L**R**	L	R	R**L**	R	L

<u>ACCENTS ARE IN BOLD AS FLAMS</u>

Day 2- Pattern - L**R** L R R**L** R L

Six Eighth Note Feet Tempo = 30 (+8)

<u>TIMING - SIX EIGHT NOTES - COUNTED AS **1** 2 3 **4** 5 6</u>

<u>GUIDE</u>

Six Eight Note Count Applied					
1	2	3	4	5	6
L**R**	L	R	R**L**	R	L

<u>ACCENTS ARE IN BOLD AS FLAMS</u>

Day 3 - Pattern - L**R** L R R**L** R L

Hand Accents Applied to Drum Numbers Tempo = 54 (+8)

TIMING - SIX EIGHT NOTES - COUNTED AS 1 2 3 4 5 6

GUIDE

The pattern L**R** L R R**L** RL is played on the snare drum (1) or any drum including hi-hat. However, every accent to be played, should be played according to the drum numbers.

THIS IS A **2** BAR PATTERN.

PLAY NOTES AS CLOSE TOGETHER AS POSSIBLE, MAINTAINING THE HAND SWAP.

Hand Drum Numbers			
1234	2341	3412	4123
1243	2314	3421	4132
1324	2134	3124	4213
1342	2143	3142	4231
1423	2413	3214	4312
1432	2431	3241	4321

Day 4 - Pattern - L**R** L R R**L** R L

Hi-Hat Hand Tempo = 54 (+8)

TIMING - SIX EIGHT NOTES - COUNTED AS 1 2 3 4 5 6

GUIDE

Play the flam accent pattern on the Hi-hat firmly closed, whilst playing steady half notes on the bass drum. Bass drum will be played on beats 1 3 5.

Accents on beat 1 and 4 should not be ignored.

Day 5 - Pattern - L**R** L R R**L** R L

Cymbal Tempo = 54 (+8)

<u>TIMING - SIX EIGHT NOTES - COUNTED AS **1** 2 3 4 5 **6**</u>

<u>GUIDE</u>

Play the flam accent pattern on the snare drum whilst positioning the accent to the crash cymbal and / or ride cymbal.

The pattern can be played as normal for multiple bars to build ambience.

Try the pattern with and without the bass drum for a variation of effects.

Day 6 - Pattern - L**R** L R R**L** R L

Eighth Note Triplet Hand Tempo = 54 (+8)

TIMING - EIGHTH NOTE TRIPLET - COUNTED AS 1 TRIP LET 2 TRIP LET 3 TRIP LET 4 TRIP LET

<u>GUIDE</u>

Eighth Note triplet Count											
1	Trip	Let	2	Trip	Let	3	Trip	Let	4	Trip	Let
L**R**	L	R	r**L**	R	L	L**R**	L	R	r**L**	R	L

BASS DRUM SHOULD PLAY STEADY QUARTER NOTES

ONCE YOU ARE COMFORTABLE WITH THE EXERCISE, APPLY TO THE DRUM NUMBERS ACROSS THE KIT AND USE AS A DRUM FILL.

Day 7 - Pattern - L**R** L R R**L** R L

Eighth Note Triplet Feet Tempo = 32 (+8)

TIMING - EIGHTH NOTE TRIPLET - COUNTED AS 1 TRIP LET 2 TRIP LET 3 TRIP LET 4 TRIP LET

GUIDE

Eighth Note triplet Count											
1	Trip	Let	2	Trip	Let	3	Trip	Let	4	Trip	Let
L**R**	L	R	r**L**	R	L	L**R**	L	R	r**L**	R	L

ONCE YOU ARE COMFORTABLE WITH THE EXERCISE, APPLY AS A DRUM FILL.

Objective - Triple Stroke Roll - Left Lead

Triple stroke roll is very much similar to the double stroke roll, however there are two major differences.

- It has 3 strokes per limb
- The timing is triplets based.

<u>CONSIDER THE DYNAMIC LEVELS AS **6** FOR THE ACCENT AND **3** FOR THE UNACCENTED, WITH NO OTHER CHANGE IN VOLUME.</u>

The pattern is **L** L L **R** R R

Beat of the Week

The drum beat will support all exercises this week. Always use a metronome at the set tempo. Keep an eye on both hands and feet while practicing to develop better technique and effective posture.

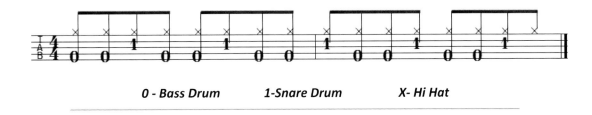

0 - Bass Drum   **1-Snare Drum**   **X- Hi Hat**

Day 1- Pattern - **L**LL**R**RR

Twelve Eighth Note Hand Tempo = 54 (+8)

TIMING - TWELVE EIGHTH NOTES - COUNTED AS 1 2 3 4 5 6 7 8 9 10 11 12

GUIDE

Basic 12-8 Count											
1	2	3	**4**	5	6	**7**	8	9	**10**	11	12
L	L	L	**R**	R	R	**L**	L	L	**R**	R	R

ACCENTS ARE IN BOLD

Day 2- Pattern - **L**LL**R**RR

Twelve Eighth Note Feet Tempo = 32 (+8)

TIMING - TWELVE EIGHTH NOTES - COUNTED AS 1 2 3 4 5 6 7 8 9 10 11 12

GUIDE

Basic 12-8 Count											
1	2	3	**4**	5	6	**7**	8	9	**10**	11	12
L	L	L	**R**	R	R	**L**	L	L	**R**	R	R

ACCENTS ARE IN BOLD

Day 3- Pattern - **L**LL**R**RR

Hand Applied to Drum Numbers Tempo = 54 (+8)

<u>TIMING - TWELVE EIGHTH NOTES - COUNTED AS **1 2 3 4 5 6 7 8 9 10 11 12**</u>

<u>GUIDE</u>

One hand per drum

An example from the table - 3 4   1 2

Drum 3 (**L**LL), Drum 4 (**R**RR), Drum 1 (**L**LL), Drum 2 (**R**RR)

Add the bass drum on each quarter note.

<u>THIS IS A **1** BAR PATTERN</u>

Hand Drum Numbers			
1234	2341	3412	4123
1243	2314	3421	4132
1324	2134	3124	4213
1342	2143	3142	4231
1423	2413	3214	4312
1432	2431	3241	4321

Day 4 - Pattern - **L**LL**R**RR

Hand Applied to Drum Numbers Tempo = 54 (+8)

TIMING - TWELVE EIGHTH NOTES - COUNTED AS 1 2 3 4 5 6 7 8 9 10 11 12

GUIDE

Three (3) drums per hand

An example from the table - 3 4 1

LH - 341

RH - 341

Add the bass drum to every third beat, 1, 4, 7, 10.

209

Hand Drum Numbers					
111	211	311	411	R11	X11
121	221	321	421	R21	X21
131	231	331	431	R31	X31
141	241	341	441	R41	X41
1R1	2R1	3R1	4R1	RR1	XR1
1X1	2X1	3X1	4X1	RX1	XX1

Day 5 - Pattern - **L**LL**R**RR

Quarter Note Triplet Hand Tempo = 54 (+8)

TIMING - QUARTER NOTE TRIPLET - COUNTED AS 1 LET TRIP 3 LET TRIP

GUIDE

Quarter Note Triplet Count											
1	Trip	Let	2	Trip	Let	**3**	Trip	Let	4	Trip	Let
x		x		x		x		x		x	
L		L		L		**R**		R		R	

ACCENTS ARE IN BOLD

210

Day 6 - Pattern - **L**LL**R**RR

Quarter Note Triplet Feet Tempo = 54 (+8)

TIMING - QUARTER NOTE TRIPLET - COUNTED AS **1** LET TRIP **3** LET TRIP

GUIDE

Quarter Note Triplet Count											
1	Trip	Let	2	Trip	Let	**3**	Trip	Let	4	Trip	Let
x		x		x		x		x		x	
L		L		L		**R**		R		R	

ACCENTS ARE IN BOLD

Day 7 - Pattern - **L**LL**R**RR

Hand Applied to Drum Numbers Tempo = 54 (+8)

TIMING - QUARTER NOTE TRIPLET - COUNTED AS **1** LET TRIP **3** LET TRIP

GUIDE

Three (3) drums per hand

An example from the table - 3 4 1

LH - 341

RH - 341

Add the bass drum to every quarter note, 1, 2, 3, 4.

212

Hand Drum Numbers					
111	211	311	411	R11	X11
121	221	321	421	R21	X21
131	231	331	431	R31	X31
141	241	341	441	R41	X41
1R1	2R1	3R1	4R1	RR1	XR1
1X1	2X1	3X1	4X1	RX1	XX1

Objective - Single Drag Tap - Right Lead

A single drag tap, also known as single drag is two alternating notes where the first note is a drag and the second is an accented single.

<u>**CONSIDER THE DYNAMIC LEVELS AS 6 FOR THE ACCENT AND 3 FOR THE UNACCENTED, WITH NO OTHER CHANGE IN VOLUME.**</u>

The pattern is LLR **L** RRL **R**.

213

Beat of the Week

The drum beat will support all exercises this week. Always use a metronome at the set tempo. Keep an eye on both hands and feet while practicing to develop better technique and effective posture.

0 - Bass Drum   **1-Snare Drum**   **X- Hi Hat**

Day 1- Pattern - LLR **L** RRL **R**

Eighth Note Hand Tempo = 54 (+8)

__TIMING - EIGHTH NOTES - COUNTED AS 1 & 2 & 3 & 4 &__

__GUIDE__

Eighth Note Count Applied											
D	1	**And**	D	2	**And**	D	3	**And**	D	4	**And**
LL	R	**L**	RR	L	**R**	LL	R	**L**	RR	L	**R**

__ACCENTS ARE IN BOLD__

Day 2 - Pattern - LLR **L** RRL **R**

Eighth Note Feet Tempo = 34 (+8)

TIMING - EIGHTH NOTES - COUNTED AS 1 & 2 & 3 & 4 &

GUIDE

Eighth Note Count Applied											
D	1	**And**	D	2	**And**	D	3	**And**	D	4	**And**
LL	R	**L**	RR	L	**R**	LL	R	**L**	RR	L	**R**

ACCENTS ARE IN BOLD

Day 3 - Pattern - LLR **L** RRL **R**

Full Hand Pattern Applied to Drum Numbers Tempo = 54 (+8)

<u>TIMING - EIGHTH NOTES - COUNTED AS **1 & 2 & 3 & 4 &**</u>

<u>GUIDE</u>

Hand application, an example from the table - 3 4 1 2

Drum 3 (LLR **L** RRL **R**), Drum 4 (LLR **L** RRL **R)**,
Drum 1 (LLR **L** RRL **R)**, Drum 2 (LLR **L** RRL **R)**

Add the bass drum on each quarter note.

<u>THIS IS A **2** BAR PATTERN</u>

Hand Drum Numbers			
1234	2341	3412	4123
1243	2314	3421	4132
1324	2134	3124	4213
1342	2143	3142	4231
1423	2413	3214	4312
1432	2431	3241	4321

Day 4 - Pattern - LLR **L** RRL **R**

Half Hand Pattern Applied to Drum Numbers Tempo = 54 (+8)

TIMING - EIGHTH NOTES - COUNTED AS **1 & 2 & 3 & 4 &**

GUIDE

Hand application, an example from the table - 3 4 1 2

    Drum 3 (LLR **L**), Drum 4 (RRL **R**), Drum 1 (LLR **L**), Drum 2 (RRL **R**)

Add the bass drum on each quarter note.

THIS IS A **1** BAR PATTERN

Hand Drum Numbers			
1234	2341	3412	4123
1243	2314	3421	4132
1324	2134	3124	4213
1342	2143	3142	4231
1423	2413	3214	4312
1432	2431	3241	4321

Day 5 - Pattern - LLR **L** RRL **R**

Split Hand D.Numbers Tempo = 54 (+8)
TIMING - EIGHTH NOTES - COUNTED AS 1 & 2 & 3 & 4 &

GUIDE

Hand application, an example from the table - 3 4

Left hand remains on the first number **(3)**, whilst Right hand remains on the second number **(4)**.

BASS DRUM SHOULD HAVE STEADY QUARTER NOTE PULSE.

Drum Numbers			
12	23	32	41
13	24	34	42
14	21	31	43
1X	2X	3X	4X

Day 6 - Pattern - LLR **L** RRL **R**

Pattern as a Beat Tempo = 54 (+8)

<u>TIMING - EIGHTH NOTES - COUNTED AS **1 & 2 & 3 & 4 &**</u>

<u>GUIDE</u>

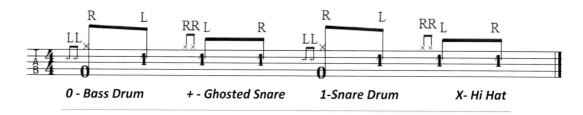

0 - Bass Drum   *+ - Ghosted Snare*   *1-Snare Drum*   *X- Hi Hat*

<u>ACCENT IS ON THE 'AND' OF EACH QUARTER NOTE</u>

Day 7 - Pattern - LLR **L** RRL **R**

Pattern as a Beat Tempo = 54 (+8)

<u>TIMING - EIGHTH NOTES - COUNTED AS 1 & 2 & 3 & 4 &</u>

<u>GUIDE</u>

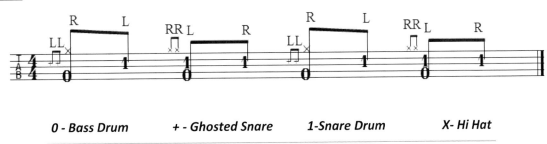

0 - Bass Drum   + - Ghosted Snare   1-Snare Drum   X- Hi Hat

<u>ACCENT IS ON THE 'AND' OF EACH QUARTER NOTE</u>

Objective - Seventeen Stroke Roll - Left Lead

Seventeen stroke roll is simple eight doubles / diddles followed by an accented note. This is not an alternating pattern but feel free to do so. **CONSIDER THE DYNAMIC LEVELS AS 6 FOR THE ACCENT AND 3 FOR THE UNACCENTED, WITH NO OTHER CHANGE IN VOLUME.**

The pattern is LLRRLLRR LLRRLLRR **L.**

Written as

Played as

222

Beat of the Week

The drum beat will support all exercises this week. Always use a metronome at the set tempo. Keep an eye on both hands and feet while practicing to develop better technique and effective posture.

0 - Bass Drum   *1-Snare Drum*   *X- Hi Hat*

Day 1- Pattern - LLRRLLRRLLRRLLRR**L**

Sixteenth Note Hand Tempo = 54 (+8)

TIMING - SIXTEENTH NOTES - COUNTED AS 1E &D 2 E & D 3 E & D 4 E & D

GUIDE

Sixteenth Note Count																			
1	E	A	D	2	E	A	D	3	E	A	D	4	E	A	D	**1**	E	A	D
L	L	R	R	L	L	R	R	L	L	R	R	L	L	R	R	**L**			
R	R	L	L	R	R	L	L	R	R	L	L	R	R	L	L	**R**			

ACCENTS ARE IN BOLD

Day 2 - Pattern - LLRRLLRRLLRRLLRRL

Sixteenth Note Feet Tempo = 24 (+8)

TIMING - SIXTEENTH NOTES - COUNTED AS 1E &D 2 E & D 3 E & D 4 E & D

GUIDE

Sixteenth Note Count																			
1	E	A	D	2	E	A	D	3	E	A	D	4	E	A	D	**1**	E	A	D
L	L	R	R	L	L	R	R	L	L	R	R	L	L	R	R	**L**			
R	R	L	L	R	R	L	L	R	R	L	L	R	R	L	L	**R**			

ACCENTS ARE IN BOLD

Day 3 - Pattern - LLRRLLRRLLRRLLRRL

Hand Pattern Applied to Drum Numbers Tempo = 54 (+8)

Timing - Sixteenth Notes - Counted as 1e &d 2 e & d 3 e & d 4 e & d

Guide

An example from the table - 3 4   1 2 C

Drum 3 (LLRR), Drum 4 (LLRR),
Drum 1 (LLRR), Drum 2 (LLRR) C (L)

Add the bass drum on each quarter note. **This is a 2 bar
pattern**

Hand Drum Numbers			
1234C	2341C	3412C	4123C
1243C	2314C	3421C	4132C
1324C	2134C	3124C	4213C
1342C	2143C	3142C	4231C
1423C	2413C	3214C	4312C
1432C	2431C	3241C	4321C

Day 4 - Pattern - LLRRLLRRLLRRLLRRL

Split Hand+Foot D.Numbers Tempo = 54 (+8)
TIMING - SIXTEENTH NOTES - COUNTED AS 1E &D 2 E & D 3 E & D 4 E & D

GUIDE

 Application,

The first number / letter will be playing represents the L part of the rudiment, whilst the second number / letter will be playing represents the R part of the rudiment. The third number represents the snare where the accent will be.

Drum Numbers			
Left Hand		Right Hand	
011	101	101	011
021	201	201	021
031	301	301	031
041	401	401	041
0X1	X01	X01	0X1
Y11	1Y1	1Y1	Y11
Y21	2Y1	2Y1	Y21
Y31	3Y1	3Y1	Y31
Y41	4Y1	4Y1	Y41
YX1	XY1	XY1	YX1

Day 5- Pattern - LLRRLLRRLLRRLLRRL

Thirty Second Note Hand Tempo = 54 (+8)

TIMING -THIRTY-SECOND NOTES - COUNTED AS 1E &D & E &D 2 E &D & E &D 3 E &D & E &D 4 E &D & E &D

GUIDE

Thirty Second Note count Applied																															
1	E	A	D	&	E	A	D	2	E	A	D	&	E	A	D	3	E	A	D	&	E	A	D	4	E	A	D	&	E	A	D
L	L	R	R	L	L	R	R	L	L	R	R	L	L	R	R	**L**															
R	R	L	L	R	R	L	L	R	R	L	L	R	R	L	L	**R**															

ACCENTS ARE IN BOLD

228

Day 6 - Pattern - LLRRLLRRLLRRLLRR**L**

Thirty Second Note Feet Tempo = 24 (+8)

TIMING -THIRTY-SECOND NOTES - COUNTED AS 1E &D & E &D 2 E &D & E &D 3 E &D & E &D 4 E &D & E &D

GUIDE

Thirty Second Note count Applied																															
1	E	A	D	&	E	A	D	2	E	A	D	&	E	A	D	3	E	A	D	&	E	A	D	4	E	A	D	&	E	A	D
L	L	R	R	L	L	R	R	L	L	R	R	L	L	R	R	**L**															
R	R	L	L	R	R	L	L	R	R	L	L	R	R	L	L	**R**															

ACCENTS ARE IN BOLD

Day 7 - Pattern - LLRRLLRRLLRRLLRRL

Hand Pattern Applied to Drum Numbers Tempo = 54 (+8)

TIMING -THIRTY-SECOND NOTES - COUNTED AS 1E &D & E &D 2 E &D & E &D 3 E &D & E &D 4 E &D & E &D

GUIDE

An example from the table - 3 4 1 2 C

Drum 3 (LLRR), Drum 4 (LLRR),
Drum 1 (LLRR), Drum 2 (LLRR) C **(L)**

Add the bass drum on each quarter note.

THIS IS A **1** BAR PATTERN, ACCENT IS ON BEAT **3**

Hand Drum Numbers			
1234C	2341C	3412C	4123C
1243C	2314C	3421C	4132C
1324C	2134C	3124C	4213C
1342C	2143C	3142C	4231C
1423C	2413C	3214C	4312C
1432C	2431C	3241C	4321C

230

Objective - Flam Tap - Right Lead

Flam tap is alternating doubles / diddles with flams on the first note of each double / diddle.

CONSIDER THE DYNAMIC LEVELS AS 6 FOR THE ACCENT AND 3 FOR THE UNACCENTED, WITH NO OTHER CHANGE IN VOLUME.

The pattern is ₗR R ᵣL L .

Beat of the Week

The drum beat will support all exercises this week. Always use a metronome at the set tempo. Keep an eye on both hands and feet while practicing to develop better technique and effective posture.

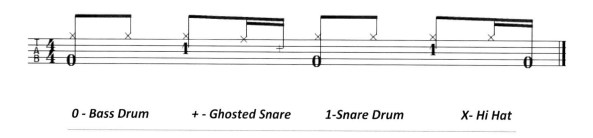

0 - Bass Drum   **+ - Ghosted Snare**   **1-Snare Drum**   **X- Hi Hat**

Day 1- Pattern - L**R** R R**L** L

Eighth Note Hand Tempo = 54 (+8)

TIMING - EIGHTH NOTES - COUNTED AS 1 & 2 & 3 & 4 &

GUIDE

Eighth Note Count Applied											
D	**1**	And	D	**2**	And	D	**3**	And	D	**4**	And
L	**R**	R	R	**L**	L	L	**R**	R	R	**L**	L

ACCENTS ARE IN BOLD

Day 2- Pattern - L**R** R R**L** L

Eighth Note Feet Tempo = 34 (+8)

<u>TIMING - EIGHTH NOTES - COUNTED AS 1 & 2 & 3 & 4 &</u>

<u>GUIDE</u>

Eighth Note Count Applied											
D	**1**	And	D	**2**	And	D	**3**	And	D	**4**	And
L	**R**	R	R	**L**	L	L	**R**	R	R	**L**	L

<u>ACCENTS ARE IN BOLD</u>

234

Day 3 - Pattern - L**R** R R**L** L

Hand Pattern Applied to Drum Numbers Tempo = 54 (+8)

TIMING - EIGHTH NOTES - COUNTED AS 1 & 2 & 3 & 4 &

GUIDE

An example from the table - 3 4 1 2

Drum 3 (L**R** R), Drum 4 (R**L** L),
Drum 1 (L**R** R), Drum 2 (R**L** L)

Add the bass drum on each quarter note.

THIS IS A 1 BAR PATTERN

Hand Drum Numbers			
1234	2341	3412	4123
1243	2314	3421	4132
1324	2134	3124	4213
1342	2143	3142	4231
1423	2413	3214	4312
1432	2431	3241	4321

Day 4- Pattern - L**R** R R**L** L

Twelve Eighth Note Hand Tempo = 54 (+8)

TIMING - TWELVE EIGHTH NOTES - COUNTED AS 1 2 3 4 5 6 7 8 9 10 11 12

GUIDE

Basic 12-8 Count											
1	2	**3**	4	**5**	6	**7**	8	**9**	10	**11**	12
L**R**	R	R**L**	L	L**R**	R	R**L**	L	L**R**	R	R**L**	L

ACCENTS ARE IN BOLD

Day 5 - Pattern - L**R** R R**L** L

Twelve Eighth Note Feet Tempo = 44 (+8)

Timing - Twelve Eighth Notes - Counted as 1 2 3 4 5 6 7 8 9 10 11 12

Guide

Basic 12-8 Count											
1	2	**3**	4	**5**	6	**7**	8	**9**	10	**11**	12
L**R**	R	R**L**	L	L**R**	R	R**L**	L	L**R**	R	R**L**	L

Accents are in bold

Day 6 - Pattern - L**R** R R**L** L

Hand Pattern Applied to Drum Numbers Tempo = 54 (+8)

<u>TIMING - TWELVE EIGHTH NOTES - COUNTED AS **1 2 3 4 5 6 7 8 9 10 11 12**</u>

<u>GUIDE</u>

An example from the table - 3 4 1 2

Drum 3 (L**R** R), Drum 4 (R**L** L),
Drum 1 (L**R** R), Drum 2 (R**L** L)

Add the bass drum on 1 4 7 10.

<u>THIS IS A **1** BAR PATTERN</u>

238

Hand Drum Numbers			
1234	2341	3412	4123
1243	2314	3421	4132
1324	2134	3124	4213
1342	2143	3142	4231
1423	2413	3214	4312
1432	2431	3241	4321

Day 7 - Pattern - L**R** R R**L** L

Hand Accents Applied to Drum Numbers Tempo = 54 (+8)

TIMING - TWELVE EIGHTH NOTES - COUNTED AS 1 2 3 4 5 6 7 8 9 10 11 12

GUIDE

The pattern L**R** R R**L** L is played on the snare drum (1) or any drum including hi-hat. However, every accent to be played, should be played according to the drum numbers.

THIS IS A **1** BAR PATTERN.

PLAY NOTES AS CLOSE TOGETHER AS POSSIBLE, MAINTAINING THE HAND SWAP.

Hand Drum Numbers			
1234	2341	3412	4123
1243	2314	3421	4132
1324	2134	3124	4213
1342	2143	3142	4231
1423	2413	3214	4312
1432	2431	3241	4321

239

Objective - Double Ratamacue - Right Lead

Double Ratamacue is a single ratamacue with a drag before it.

<u>CONSIDER THE DYNAMIC LEVELS AS **6** FOR THE ACCENT AND **3** FOR THE UNACCENTED, WITH NO OTHER CHANGE IN VOLUME.</u>

The pattern is _{LL}R _{LL}R L R L **L** _{RR}L _{RR}L R L **R**

Beat of the Week

The drum beat will support all exercises this week. Always use a metronome at the set tempo. Keep an eye on both hands and feet while practicing to develop better technique and effective posture.

0 - Bass Drum   1-Snare Drum   X- Hi Hat

Day 1- Pattern-LLR LLR L R **L** RRL RRL R L **R**

Six Eighth Note Hand Tempo = 54 (+8)

<u>TIMING - SIX EIGHT NOTES - COUNTED AS **1 2 3 4 5 6**</u>

<u>GUIDE</u>

Six Eighth Count Applied										
1	2	Trip	Let	**3**	4	5	Trip	Let	**6**
LL R	LL R	L	R	**L**	RR L	RR L	R	L	**R**

<u>ACCENTS ARE IN BOLD</u>

Day 2- Pattern-LLR LLR L R **L** RRL RRLR L **R**

Six Eighth Note Feet Tempo = 44 (+8)

<u>Timing - Six Eight Notes - Counted as 1 2 3 4 5 6</u>

<u>Guide</u>

Six Eighth Count Applied									
1	2	Trip	Let	**3**	4	5	Trip	Let	**6**
LL R	LL R	L	R	**L**	RR L	RR L	R	L	**R**

<u>Accents are in bold</u>

Day 3- Pattern-LLR LLR L R **L** RRL RRL R L **R**

Full Hand Pattern Applied to Drum Numbers Tempo = 54 (+8)

TIMING - SIX EIGHT NOTES - COUNTED AS 1 2 3 4 5 6

GUIDE

Hand application, an example from the table - 3 4 1 2

Drum 3 (LLR LLR L R **L** RRL RRL R L **R**),

Drum 4 (LLR LLR L R **L** RRL RRL R L **R)** and so on

THIS IS A 4 BAR PATTERN

Hand Drum Numbers			
1234	2341	3412	4123
1243	2314	3421	4132
1324	2134	3124	4213
1342	2143	3142	4231
1423	2413	3214	4312
1432	2431	3241	4321

Day 4- Pattern-LLR LLR L R **L** RRL RRL R L **R**

Hand Accents Applied to Drum Numbers Tempo = 54 (+8)

<u>TIMING - SIX EIGHT NOTES - COUNTED AS **1 2 3 4 5 6**</u>

<u>GUIDE</u>

The pattern *LLR LLR LR **L** RRL RRL R L **R*** is played on the snare drum (1) or any drum including hi-hat. However, every accent to be played, should be played according to the drum numbers.

<u>THIS IS A **2** BAR PATTERN</u>.

<u>PLAY NOTES AS CLOSE TOGETHER AS POSSIBLE, MAINTAINING THE HAND SWAP</u>.

245

Hand Drum Numbers			
1234	2341	3412	4123
1243	2314	3421	4132
1324	2134	3124	4213
1342	2143	3142	4231
1423	2413	3214	4312
1432	2431	3241	4321

Day 5- Pattern-LLR LLR L R **L** RRL RRL R L **R**

Split Hand + Foot D.Numbers Tempo = 54 (+8)
TIMING - SIX EIGHT NOTES - COUNTED AS **1 2 3 4 5 6**

 GUIDE

 Application,

The first number / letter will be playing represents the L part of the rudiment, whilst the second number / letter will be playing represents the R part of the rudiment.

Drum Numbers			
Left Hand		Right Hand	
01	10	10	01
02	20	20	02
03	30	30	03
04	40	40	04
0X	X0	X0	0X
Y1	1Y	1Y	Y1
Y2	2Y	2Y	Y2
Y3	3Y	3Y	Y3
Y4	4Y	4Y	Y4
YX	XY	XY	YX

Day 6- Pattern-LLR LLR L R **L** RRL RRL R L **R**

Cymbal Tempo = 54 (+8)

<u>TIMING - SIX EIGHT NOTES - COUNTED AS **1 2 3 4 5 6**</u>

<u>GUIDE</u>

Play the double Ratamacue pattern on the one crash cymbal or multiple cymbals at the end of a fill, crashing on accent of 3 and 6.

The pattern can be played as normal for multiple bars to build ambience in a ballad song.

Try the pattern with and without the bass drum for a variation of effects.

Day 7- Pattern-LLR LLR L R **L** RRL RRL R L **R**

Hi-Hat Hand Tempo = 54 (+8)

TIMING - SIX EIGHT NOTES - COUNTED AS 1 2 3 4 5 6

GUIDE

Play the double Ratamacue pattern on the hi-hat firmly closed, whilst playing steady quarter notes on the bass drum. Start slow making sure the accents are correctly placed.   Make sure not to play the bass drum along with the doubles strokes.

Bass drum will be on beat 1 2 3 4 5 6.

Objective-Freestyle Mix of Past Rudiments

Mix all the various exercises we have learnt into a variety of combinations as follows, using daily application method daily.

Day	Rudiments To Mix	Daily Application Method
1	5 Stroke Roll + Ratamacue	Hands
2	Flam Drag + Flam Accent	Feet
3	Triple Stroke Roll + Single Drag Tap	Split Limbs
4	Flam + 17 Stroke Roll	Across Drum Numbers
5	Flam Tap + Double Ratamacue	Accent Across Drum Numbers
6	Ratamacue + Double Ratamacue	Accent On Snare Drum
7	Flam Tap + Flam Drag	Across Cymbals

Keep an eye on both hands and feet while practicing to develop better technique.

Objective - Single Stroke 7 - Right Lead

Single stroke seven is 7 notes played with an alternating sticking as sextuplets followed by a quarter note accent .

CONSIDER THE DYNAMIC LEVELS AS 6 FOR THE ACCENT AND 3 FOR THE UNACCENTED, WITH NO OTHER CHANGE IN VOLUME.

The pattern is RLRLRL**R** LRLRLR**L**

Beat of the Week

The drum beat will support all exercises this week. Always use a metronome at the set tempo. Keep an eye on both hands and feet while practicing to develop better technique and effective posture.

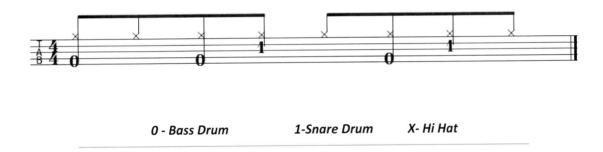

0 - Bass Drum   *1-Snare Drum*   *X- Hi Hat*

Day 1- Pattern-RLRLRL**R** LRLRLR**L**

Thirty Second Note Hand Tempo = 54 (+8)

TIMING -THIRTY-SECOND NOTES - COUNTED AS 1E &D & E &D 2 E &D & E &D 3 E &D & E &D 4 E &D & E &D

GUIDE

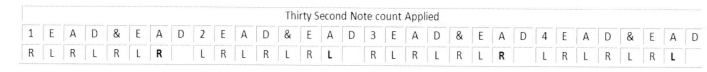

												Thirty Second Note count Applied																			
1	E	A	D	&	E	A	D	2	E	A	D	&	E	A	D	3	E	A	D	&	E	A	D	4	E	A	D	&	E	A	D
R	L	R	L	R	L	**R**		L	R	L	R	L	R	**L**		R	L	R	L	R	L	**R**		L	R	L	R	L	R	**L**	

ACCENTS ARE IN BOLD

Day 2- Pattern-RLRLRL**R** LRLRLR**L**

Thirty Second Note Feet Tempo = 24 (+8)

<u>TIMING -THIRTY-SECOND NOTES - COUNTED AS 1E &D & E &D 2 E &D & E &D 3 E &D & E &D 4 E &D & E &D</u>

<u>GUIDE</u>

Thirty Second Note count Applied																															
1	E	A	D	&	E	A	D	2	E	A	D	&	E	A	D	3	E	A	D	&	E	A	D	4	E	A	D	&	E	A	D
R	L	R	L	R	L	**R**		L	R	L	R	L	R	**L**		R	L	R	L	R	L	**R**		L	R	L	R	L	R	**L**	

<u>ACCENTS ARE IN BOLD</u>

Day 3- Pattern-RLRLRL**R** LRLRLR**L**

Full Hand Pattern Applied to Drum Numbers Tempo = 54 (+8)

TIMING -THIRTY-SECOND NOTES - COUNTED AS 1E &D & E &D 2 E &D & E &D 3 E &D & E &D 4 E &D & E &D

GUIDE

Hand application, an example from the table - 3 4 1 2

Drum 3 (RLRLRL**R** LRLRLR**L**), Drum 4 (RLRLRL**R** LRLRLR**L**),
Drum 1 (RLRLRL**R** LRLRLR**L**), Drum 2(RLRLRL**R** LRLRLR**L**)

THIS IS A **1** BAR PATTERN

Hand Drum Numbers			
1234	2341	3412	4123
1243	2314	3421	4132
1324	2134	3124	4213
1342	2143	3142	4231
1423	2413	3214	4312
1432	2431	3241	4321

Day 4- Pattern-RLRLRL**R** LRLRLR**L**

Hand Accents Applied to Drum Numbers Tempo = 54 (+8)

TIMING -THIRTY-SECOND NOTES - COUNTED AS 1E &D & E &D & E &D 2 E &D & E &D 3 E &D & E &D 4 E &D & E &D

GUIDE

The pattern RLRLRL**R** LRLRLR**L** is played on the snare drum (1) or any drum including hi-hat. However, every accent to be played, should be played according to the drum numbers.

PLAY NOTES AS CLOSE TOGETHER AS POSSIBLE, MAINTAINING THE HAND SWAP.

THIS IS A **1** BAR PATTERN.

Hand Drum Numbers			
1234	2341	3412	4123
1243	2314	3421	4132
1324	2134	3124	4213
1342	2143	3142	4231
1423	2413	3214	4312
1432	2431	3241	4321

Day 5- Pattern-RLRLRL**R** LRLRLR**L**

Sixteenth Note Triplet Hand Tempo = 54 (+8)

TIMING - SIXTEENTH NOTES - COUNTED AS 1 TRIP LET AND TRIP LET 2 TRIP LET AND TRIP LET 3 TRIP LET AND TRIP LET 4 TRIP LET AND TRIP LET

<u>GUIDE</u>

Sixteenth Note triplet Count																							
1	T	L	&	T	L	2	T	L	&	T	L	3	T	L	&	T	L	4	T	L	&	T	L
R	L	R	L	R	L	**R**							L	R	L	R	L	R	**L**					

<u>ACCENTS ARE IN BOLD</u>

Day 6 - Pattern-RLRLRL**R** LRLRLR**L**

Sixteenth Note Triplet Feet Tempo = 34 (+8)

TIMING - SIXTEENTH NOTES - COUNTED AS **1** TRIP LET AND TRIP LET **2** TRIP LET AND TRIP LET **3** TRIP LET AND TRIP LET **4** TRIP LET AND TRIP LET

GUIDE

Sixteenth Note triplet Count																							
1	T	L	&	T	L	2	T	L	&	T	L	3	T	L	&	T	L	4	T	L	&	T	L
R	L	R	L	R	L	**R**						L	R	L	R	L	R	**L**					

ACCENTS ARE IN BOLD

257

Day 7- Pattern-RLRLRL**R** LRLRLR**L**

Full Hand Pattern Applied to Drum Numbers Tempo = 54 (+8)

TIMING - SIXTEENTH NOTES - COUNTED AS 1 TRIP LET AND TRIP LET 2 TRIP LET AND TRIP LET 3 TRIP LET AND TRIP LET 4 TRIP LET AND TRIP LET

GUIDE

Hand application, an example from the table - 3 4 1 2

Drum 3 (RLRLRL**R** LRLRLR**L**), Drum 4 (RLRLRL**R** LRLRLR**L**),
Drum 1 (RLRLRL**R** LRLRLR**L**), Drum 2(RLRLRL**R** LRLRLR**L**)

THIS IS A **2** BAR PATTERN

Hand Drum Numbers			
1234	2341	3412	4123
1243	2314	3421	4132
1324	2134	3124	4213
1342	2143	3142	4231
1423	2413	3214	4312
1432	2431	3241	4321

Objective - Flam Paradiddle - Right Lead

Flam paradiddle is a paradiddle with a flam on the first note. Also known as a 'Flamadiddle'. This is an alternating rudiment.

CONSIDER THE DYNAMIC LEVELS AS **6** FOR THE ACCENT AND **3** FOR THE UNACCENTED, WITH NO OTHER CHANGE IN VOLUME.

The pattern is ₗ**R** L RR ᵣ**L** R L L

Beat of the Week

The drum beat will support all exercises this week. Always use a metronome at the set tempo. Keep an eye on both hands and feet while practicing to develop better technique and effective posture.

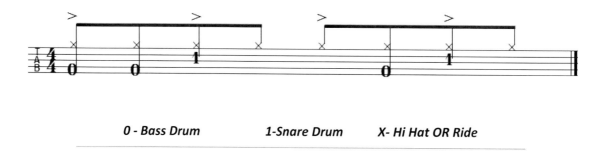

0 - Bass Drum   **1-Snare Drum**   **X- Hi Hat OR Ride**

Day 1- Pattern- L**R** L R R R**L** R L L

Eighth Note Hand Tempo = 54 (+8)

TIMING - EIGHTH NOTES - COUNTED AS 1 & 2 & 3 & 4 &

GUIDE

Eighth Note Count Applied							
1	And	2	And	3	And	4	And
L**R**	L	R	R	R**L**	R	L	L

ACCENTS ARE IN BOLD

Day 2- Pattern- L**R** L R R R**L** R L L

Eighth Note Feet Tempo = 34 (+8)

TIMING - EIGHTH NOTES - COUNTED AS 1 & 2 & 3 & 4 &

GUIDE

Eighth Note Count Applied							
1	And	2	And	**3**	And	4	And
L**R**	L	R	R	**RL**	R	L	L

ACCENTS ARE IN BOLD

Day 3- Pattern- L**R** L R R R**L** R L L

Full Hand Pattern Applied to Drum Numbers Tempo = 54 (+8)

TIMING - EIGHTH NOTES - COUNTED AS 1 & 2 & 3 & 4 &

GUIDE

Hand application, an example from the table - 3 4 1 2

Drum 3 (L**R**LRR R**L**RLL), Drum 4 (L**R**LRR R**L**RLL),
Drum 1 (L**R**LRR R**L**RLL), Drum 2 (L**R**LRR R**L**RLL)

THIS IS A **4** BAR PATTERN

Hand Drum Numbers			
1234	2341	3412	4123
1243	2314	3421	4132
1324	2134	3124	4213
1342	2143	3142	4231
1423	2413	3214	4312
1432	2431	3241	4321

Day 4- Pattern- L**R** L R R R**L** R L L

Hand Accents Applied to Drum Numbers Tempo = 54 (+8)

<u>TIMING - EIGHTH NOTES - COUNTED AS 1 & 2 & 3 & 4 &</u>

<u>GUIDE</u>

The pattern (L**R**LRR RLRLL) is played on the snare drum (1) or any drum including hi-hat. However, every accent to be played, should be played according to the drum numbers.

PLAY NOTES AS CLOSE TOGETHER AS POSSIBLE, MAINTAINING THE HAND SWAP.

<u>THIS IS A **2** BAR PATTERN</u>

Hand Drum Numbers			
1234	2341	3412	4123
1243	2314	3421	4132
1324	2134	3124	4213
1342	2143	3142	4231
1423	2413	3214	4312
1432	2431	3241	4321

Day 5 - Pattern- L**R** L R R R**L** R L L

Split Hand + Foot D.Numbers Tempo = 54 (+8)
TIMING - EIGHTH NOTES - COUNTED AS 1 & 2 & 3 & 4 &

GUIDE

Application,

The first number / letter will be playing represents the L part of the rudiment, whilst the second number / letter will be playing represents the R part of the rudiment. The third number represents the snare where the accent will be.

Drum Numbers			
Left Hand		Right Hand	
011	101	101	011
021	201	201	021
031	301	301	031
041	401	401	041
0X1	X01	X01	0X1
Y11	1Y1	1Y1	Y11
Y21	2Y1	2Y1	Y21
Y31	3Y1	3Y1	Y31
Y41	4Y1	4Y1	Y41
YX1	XY1	XY1	YX1

265

Day 6 - Pattern - L**R** L R R R**L** R L L

Sixteenth Note Hand Tempo = 54 (+8)

TIMING - SIXTEENTH NOTES - COUNTED AS 1E &D 2 E & D 3 E & D 4 E & D

GUIDE

Sixteenth Note Count Applied															
1	E	&	D	**2**	E	&	D	**3**	E	&	D	**4**	E	&	D
LR	L	R	R	RL	R	L	L	LR	L	R	R	RL	R	L	L

ONCE ACHIEVED, APPLY TO DRUM NUMBERS WITH EACH QUARTER NOTE VALUE ON ONE DRUM SURFACE.

Day 7 - Pattern - L**R** L R R R**L** R L L

Hand Pattern with Bass Drum Tempo = 54 (+8)

TIMING - SIXTEENTH NOTES - COUNTED AS 1E &D 2 E & D 3 E & D 4 E & D

GUIDE

Sixteenth Note Count Applied															
1	E	&	D	2	E	&	D	3	E	&	D	4	E	&	D
LR	L	R	R	RL	R	L	L	LR	L	R	R	RL	R	L	L

SAME AS YESTERDAY, 5 STROKES PER DRUM SURFACE. HOWEVER, BASS DRUM SHOULD BE INCLUDED ON THE AND OF 2 + THE AND OF 4.

Objective - 11 Stroke Roll - Right Lead

Eleven stroke roll is 5 doubles/diddles followed by an accented note.

CONSIDER THE DYNAMIC LEVELS AS **6** FOR THE ACCENT AND **3** FOR THE UNACCENTED, WITH NO OTHER CHANGE IN VOLUME.

The pattern is RRLLRRLLRR**L**

Beat of the Week

The drum beat will support all exercises this week. Always use a metronome at the set tempo. Keep an eye on both hands and feet while practicing to develop better technique and effective posture.

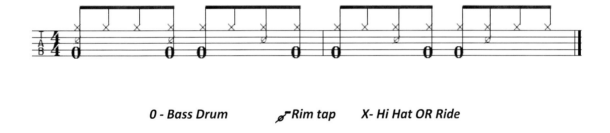

0 - Bass Drum   *Rim tap*   *X- Hi Hat OR Ride*

Day 1 - Pattern - RRLLRRLLRR**L**

Sixteenth Note Hand Tempo = 54 (+8)

TIMING - SIXTEENTH NOTES - COUNTED AS **1** E **&** D **2** E **&** D **3** E **&** D **4** E **&** D

GUIDE

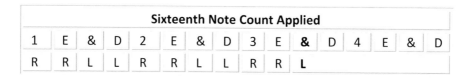

ONCE ACHIEVED, APPLY THE BASS DRUM TO QUARTER NOTES - **1 2 3 4.**

Day 2 - Pattern - RRLLRRLLRRL

Sixteenth Note Feet Tempo = 34 (+8)

TIMING - SIXTEENTH NOTES - COUNTED AS 1E &D 2 E & D 3 E & D 4 E & D

GUIDE

Sixteenth Note Count Applied															
1	E	&	D	2	E	&	D	3	E	&	D	4	E	&	D
R	R	L	L	R	R	L	L	R	R	**L**					

SWITCH BETWEEN PLAYING QUARTER NOTES AND EIGHTH NOTES ON EITHER HAND.

Day 3 - Pattern - RRLLRRLLRRL

Split Hand Pattern Applied to Drum Numbers Tempo = 54 (+8)

TIMING - SIXTEENTH NOTES - COUNTED AS 1E &D 2 E & D 3 E & D 4 E & D

GUIDE

Hand application, an example from the table - 3 2 1
Drum 3 (RRLL), Drum 2 (RRLL), Drum 1 (RR**L**)

THIS IS A **1** BAR PATTERN

3 Hand Drum Numbers						
111	211	311	411	R11	X11	C11
121	221	321	421	R21	X21	C21
131	231	331	431	R31	X31	C31
141	241	341	441	R41	X41	C41
1R1	2R1	3R1	4R1	RR1	XR1	CR1
1X1	2X1	3X1	4X1	RX1	XX1	CX1

272

Day 4 - Pattern - RRLLRRLLRRL

Hand Pattern with Bass to Drum Numbers Tempo = 54 (+8)

TIMING - SIXTEENTH NOTES - COUNTED AS 1E &D 2 E & D 3 E & D 4 E & D

GUIDE

Hand application, an example from the table - 3 2 1
Drum 3 (RRLL), Drum 2 (RRLL), Drum 1 (RRL)

Once comfortable with the pattern applied to the numbers,
the Bass drum should be added on beats '4' + 'And' at the
end of the pattern.

THIS IS A 1 BAR PATTERN

3 Hand Drum Numbers						
111	211	311	411	R11	X11	C11
121	221	321	421	R21	X21	C21
131	231	331	431	R31	X31	C31
141	241	341	441	R41	X41	C41
1R1	2R1	3R1	4R1	RR1	XR1	CR1
1X1	2X1	3X1	4X1	RX1	XX1	CX1

Day 5 - Pattern - RRLLRRLLRRL

Split Hand+Foot D.Numbers Tempo = 54 (+8)

TIMING - SIXTEENTH NOTES - COUNTED AS 1E &D 2 E & D 3 E & D 4 E & D

GUIDE

Application,

The first number / letter will be playing represents the L part of the rudiment, whilst the second number / letter will be playing represents the R part of the rudiment. The third number represents the snare where the accent will be.

Drum Numbers			
Left Hand		Right Hand	
011	101	101	011
021	201	201	021
031	301	301	031
041	401	401	041
0X1	X01	X01	0X1
Y11	1Y1	1Y1	Y11
Y21	2Y1	2Y1	Y21
Y31	3Y1	3Y1	Y31
Y41	4Y1	4Y1	Y41
YX1	XY1	XY1	YX1

Day 6 - Pattern - RRLLRRLLRR**L**

Thirty Second Note Hand Tempo = 54 (+8)

TIMING -THIRTY-SECOND NOTES - COUNTED AS 1E &D & E &D 2 E &D & E &D 3 E &D & E &D 4 E &D & E &D

<u>GUIDE</u>

Thirty Second Note count Applied																															
1	E	A	D	&	E	A	D	2	E	A	D	&	E	A	D	3	E	A	D	&	E	A	D	4	E	A	D	&	E	A	D
R	R	L	L	R	R	L	L	R	R	**L**						R	R	L	L	R	R	L	L	R	R	**L**					

<u>ACCENTS ARE IN BOLD</u>

275

Day 7 - Pattern - RRLLRRLLRR**L**

Thirty Second Note Feet Tempo = 24 (+8)

TIMING -THIRTY-SECOND NOTES - COUNTED AS 1E &D & E &D 2 E &D & E &D 3 E &D & E &D 4 E &D & E &D

GUIDE

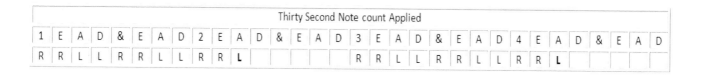

Thirty Second Note count Applied																															
1	E	A	D	&	E	A	D	2	E	A	D	&	E	A	D	3	E	A	D	&	E	A	D	4	E	A	D	&	E	A	D
R	R	L	L	R	R	L	L	R	R	**L**					R	R	R	L	L	R	R	L	L	R	R	**L**					

ACCENTS ARE IN BOLD

276

Objective - 15 Stroke Roll - Right Lead

Fifteen stroke roll is 7 doubles / diddles followed by an accented note.

CONSIDER THE DYNAMIC LEVELS AS **6** FOR THE ACCENT AND **3** FOR THE UNACCENTED, WITH NO OTHER CHANGE IN VOLUME.

The pattern is RRLLRRLLRRLLRR**L**.

Beat of the Week

The drum beat will support all exercises this week. Always use a metronome at the set tempo. Keep an eye on both hands and feet while practicing to develop better technique and effective posture.

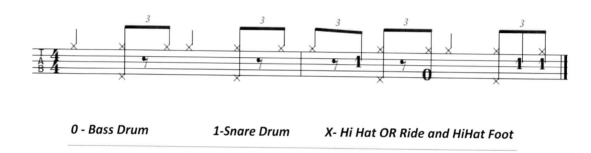

0 - Bass Drum *1-Snare Drum* *X- Hi Hat OR Ride and HiHat Foot*

Day 1 - Pattern - RRLLRRLLRRLLRRL

Sixteenth Note Hand Tempo = 54 (+8)

TIMING - SIXTEENTH NOTES - COUNTED AS 1E &D 2 E & D 3 E & D 4 E & D

GUIDE

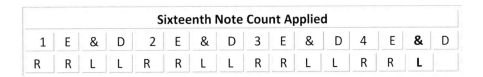

Sixteenth Note Count Applied															
1	E	&	D	2	E	&	D	3	E	&	D	4	E	&	D
R	R	L	L	R	R	L	L	R	R	L	L	R	R	L	

ONCE ACHIEVED, APPLY THE BASS DRUM TO QUARTER NOTES - 1 2 3 4.

Day 2 - Pattern - RRLLRRLLRRLLRRL

Sixteenth Note Feet Tempo = 34 (+8)

TIMING - SIXTEENTH NOTES - COUNTED AS 1E &D 2 E & D 3 E & D 4 E & D

GUIDE

Sixteenth Note Count Applied															
1	E	&	D	2	E	&	D	3	E	&	D	4	E	&	D
R	R	L	L	R	R	L	L	R	R	L	L	R	R	L	

SWITCH BETWEEN PLAYING QUARTER NOTES AND EIGHTH NOTES ON EITHER HAND.

Day 3 - Pattern - RRLLRRLLRRLLRR**L**

Hand Pattern Applied to Drum Numbers Tempo = 54 (+8)

TIMING - EIGHTH NOTES - COUNTED AS **1 & 2 & 3 & 4 &**

GUIDE

An example from the table - 3 4 1 2

Drum 3 (RRLL), Drum 4 (RRLL), Drum 1 (RRLL), Drum 2 (RR**L**)

Add the bass drum on each quarter note.

THIS IS A **1** BAR PATTERN

Hand Drum Numbers			
1234	2341	3412	4123
1243	2314	3421	4132
1324	2134	3124	4213
1342	2143	3142	4231
1423	2413	3214	4312
1432	2431	3241	4321

Day 4 - Pattern - RRLLRRLLRRLLRRL

Hand Pattern Applied to DN, Accent On Snare Tempo = 54 (+8)

TIMING - EIGHTH NOTES - COUNTED AS 1 & 2 & 3 & 4 &

GUIDE

An example from the table - 3 4 1 2 1

Drum 3 (RRLL), Drum 4 (RRLL), Drum 1 (RRLL),
Drum 2 (RR) Drum 1 (L)

Add the bass drum on each quarter note.

THIS IS A 1 BAR PATTERN

282

Hand Drum Numbers			
12341	23411	34121	41231
12431	23141	34211	41321
13241	21341	31241	42131
13421	21431	31421	42311
14231	24131	32141	43121
14321	24311	32411	43211

Day 5 - Pattern - RRLLRRLLRRLLRR**L**

Hand Pattern with Bass to Drum Numbers Tempo = 54 (+8)

TIMING - SIXTEENTH NOTES - COUNTED AS 1E &D 2 E & D 3 E & D 4 E & D

GUIDE

Hand application, an example from the table - 3 2 1 4

Drum 3 (RRLL)**,** Drum 2 (RRLL)**,** Drum 1 (RRLL) Drum 4 (RR**L**)

The Bass drum is to be added on the 'D' of 4, after the pattern.

THIS IS A **1** BAR PATTERN

Hand Drum Numbers			
1234	2341	3412	4123
1243	2314	3421	4132
1324	2134	3124	4213
1342	2143	3142	4231
1423	2413	3214	4312
1432	2431	3241	4321

Day 6 - Pattern - RRLLRRLLRRLLRR**L**

Thirty Second Note Hand Tempo = 54 (+8)

TIMING -THIRTY-SECOND NOTES - COUNTED AS 1E &D & E &D 2 E &D & E &D 3 E &D & E &D 4 E &D & E &D

GUIDE

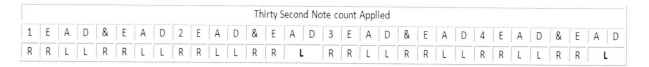

Thirty Second Note count Applied																															
1	E	A	D	&	E	A	D	2	E	A	D	&	E	A	D	3	E	A	D	&	E	A	D	4	E	A	D	&	E	A	D
R	R	L	L	R	R	L	L	R	R	L	L	R	R	**L**		R	R	L	L	R	R	L	L	R	R	L	L	R	R		**L**

ACCENTS ARE IN BOLD

Day 7 - Pattern - RRLLRRLLRRLLRR**L**

Thirty Second Note Feet Tempo = 24 (+8)

TIMING -THIRTY-SECOND NOTES - COUNTED AS 1E &D & E &D 2 E &D & E &D 3 E &D & E &D 4 E &D & E &D

GUIDE

Thirty Second Note count Applied																															
1	E	A	D	&	E	A	D	2	E	A	D	&	E	A	D	3	E	A	D	&	E	A	D	4	E	A	D	&	E	A	D
R	R	L	L	R	R	L	L	R	R	L	L	R	R	**L**	R	R	L	L	R	R	L	L	R	R	L	L	R	R	**L**		

ACCENTS ARE IN BOLD

285

Objective-Freestyle Mix of Past Rudiments

Mix all the various exercises we have learnt into a variety of combinations as follows, using daily application method daily.

Day	Rudiments To Mix	Daily Application Method
1	Single stroke 7 + Flam Accent	Hands
2	Flam Paradiddle + Flam	Feet
3	15 Stroke Roll + Single Ratamacue	Split Limbs
4	Double Ratamacue + 5 Stroke Roll	Across Drum Numbers
5	Pataflafla + Drag	Accent Across Drum Numbers
6	11 Stroke Roll + Pataflafla	Accent On Snare Drum
7	Ratamacue + Paradiddle	Across Cymbals

Keep an eye on both hands and feet while practicing to develop better technique.

Objective - 7 Stroke Roll - Right Lead

Seven stroke roll is 3 doubles / diddles as sextuplet followed by an accented quarter note.

CONSIDER THE DYNAMIC LEVELS AS 6 FOR THE ACCENT AND 3 FOR THE UNACCENTED, WITH NO OTHER CHANGE IN VOLUME.

The pattern is RRLLRR**L**

Beat of the Week

The drum beat will support all exercises this week. Always use a metronome at the set tempo. Keep an eye on both hands and feet while practicing to develop better technique and effective posture.

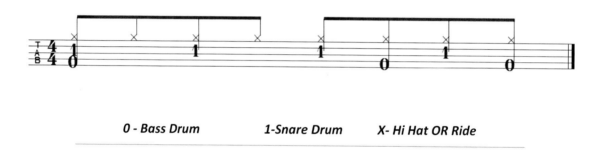

0 - Bass Drum   **1-Snare Drum**   **X- Hi Hat OR Ride**

Day 1 - Pattern - R R L L R R **L**

Eighth Note Hand Tempo = 54 (+8)

TIMING - EIGHTH NOTES - COUNTED AS 1 & 2 & 3 & 4 &

GUIDE

Eighth Note Count Applied							
1	And	2	And	3	And	**4**	And
R	R	L	L	R	R	**L**	

Maintain equal volume throughout especially on Beat 1.

Day 2 - Pattern - R R L L R R **L**

Eighth Note Feet Tempo = 54 (+6)

TIMING - EIGHTH NOTES - COUNTED AS 1 & 2 & 3 & 4 &

Eighth Note Count Applied							
1	And	2	And	3	And	**4**	And
R	R	L	L	R	R	**L**	

Maintain equal volume throughout especially on Beat 1. There is a strong possibility your right foot will play accents, Control it.

REMEMBER, THERE IS NO CHANGE IN VOLUME EXCEPT ON THE ACCENT.

Day 3 - Pattern - R R L L R R **L**

Split Hand Pattern Applied to Drum Numbers Tempo = 54 (+8)

TIMING - EIGHTH NOTES - COUNTED AS 1 & 2 & 3 & 4 &

GUIDE

An example from the table - 3 4 1 2

Drum 3 (RR), Drum 4 (LL), Drum 1 (RR), Drum 2 **(L)**

Add the bass drum on each quarter note.

THIS IS A **1** BAR PATTERN

Hand Drum Numbers			
1234	2341	3412	4123
1243	2314	3421	4132
1324	2134	3124	4213
1342	2143	3142	4231
1423	2413	3214	4312
1432	2431	3241	4321

Day 4 - Pattern - R R L L R R **L**

Sixteenth Note Hand Tempo = 54 (+8)

TIMING - SIXTEENTH NOTES TRIPLET - COUNTED AS - **1** TRIP LET AND TRIP LET **2** TRIP LET AND TRIP LET **3** TRIP LET AND TRIP LET **4** TRIP LET AND TRIP LET

GUIDE

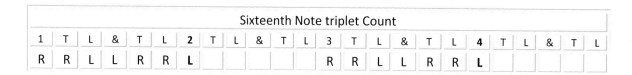

Sixteenth Note triplet Count																							
1	T	L	&	T	L	2	T	L	&	T	L	3	T	L	&	T	L	4	T	L	&	T	L
R	R	L	L	R	R	**L**						R	R	L	L	R	R	**L**					

ACCENTS ARE IN BOLD

292

Sixteenth Note Feet Tempo = 30 (+8)

TIMING - SIXTEENTH NOTES TRIPLET - COUNTED AS - **1** TRIP LET AND TRIP LET **2** TRIP LET AND TRIP LET **3** TRIP LET AND TRIP LET **4** TRIP LET AND TRIP LET

GUIDE

Sixteenth Note triplet Count																							
1	T	L	&	T	L	**2**	T	L	&	T	L	3	T	L	&	T	L	**4**	T	L	&	T	L
R	R	L	L	R	R	**L**						R	R	L	L	R	R	**L**					

ACCENTS ARE IN BOLD

Day 6 - Pattern - R R L L R R **L**

Full Hand Pattern Applied to Drum Numbers Tempo = 54 (+8)

TIMING - SIXTEENTH NOTES TRIPLET - COUNTED AS - 1 TRIP LET AND TRIP LET 2 TRIP LET AND TRIP LET 3 TRIP LET AND TRIP LET 4 TRIP LET AND TRIP LET

GUIDE

Hand application, an example from the table - 3 4 1 2

Drum 3 (RRLLRRL**L**), Drum 4 (RRLLRRL**L**),
Drum 1 (RRLLRRL**L**), Drum 2(RRLLRRL**L**)

THIS IS A **2** BAR PATTERN

Hand Drum Numbers			
1234	2341	3412	4123
1243	2314	3421	4132
1324	2134	3124	4213
1342	2143	3142	4231
1423	2413	3214	4312
1432	2431	3241	4321

Day 7- Pattern- R R L L R R **L**

Hand Accents Applied to Drum Numbers Tempo = 54 (+8)

TIMING - SIXTEENTH NOTES TRIPLET - COUNTED AS - 1 TRIP LET AND TRIP LET 2 TRIP LET AND TRIP LET 3 TRIP LET AND TRIP LET 4 TRIP LET AND TRIP LET

GUIDE

The pattern RLRLRL**R** LRLRLR**L** is played on the hi-hat or any drum including snare drum. However, every accent to be played, should be played according to the drum numbers.

THIS IS A **1** BAR PATTERN. PLAY NOTES AS CLOSE TOGETHER AS POSSIBLE, BASS DRUM PLAYING ALL QUARTER NOTES.

Hand Drum Numbers			
1234	2341	3412	4123
1243	2314	3421	4132
1324	2134	3124	4213
1342	2143	3142	4231
1423	2413	3214	4312
1432	2431	3241	4321

Objective - Single Dragadiddle Left Lead

Single Dragadiddle also known as flam paradiddle, which is a paradiddle with a flam on the first note. This is an alternating rudiment.

CONSIDER THE DYNAMIC LEVELS AS 6 FOR THE ACCENT AND 3 FOR THE UNACCENTED, WITH NO OTHER CHANGE IN VOLUME.

The pattern is LLRLL RRLRR

Beat of the Week

The drum beat will support all exercises this week. Always use a metronome at the set tempo. Keep an eye on both hands and feet while practicing to develop better technique and effective posture.

0 - Bass Drum   1-Snare Drum   X- Hi Hat OR Ride

Day 1 - Pattern - L**L** R L L R**R** L R R

Eighth Note Hand Tempo = 54 (+8)

TIMING - EIGHTH NOTES - COUNTED AS 1 & 2 & 3 & 4 &

GUIDE

Eighth Note Count Applied							
1	And	**2**	And	**3**	And	**4**	And
L**L**	R	L	L	R**R**	L	R	R

MAINTAIN **ACCENT 1** AND **3** ON THE DOUBLES.

Day 2 - Pattern - LL R L L RR L R R

Eighth Note Feet Tempo = 48 (+6)

TIMING - EIGHTH NOTES - COUNTED AS 1 & 2 & 3 & 4 &

Eighth Note Count Applied							
1	And	2	And	**3**	And	4	And
LL	R	L	L	RR	L	R	R

Maintain equal volume throughout especially on Beat 1. There is a strong possibility your right foot will play unwanted accents, Control it.

REMEMBER, THERE IS NO CHANGE IN VOLUME EXCEPT ON THE ACCENT.

Day 3 - Pattern - LL R L L RR L R R

Hi-Hat Hand Tempo = 54 (+8)
TIMING - EIGHTH NOTES - COUNTED AS 1 & 2 & 3 & 4 &

GUIDE

Play the single Dragadiddle pattern on the hi-hat firmly closed, whilst playing steady quarter notes on the bass drum. Start slow making sure the accents are correctly placed.

Make sure to play the bass drum along with the second double stroke note on beats 1 and 3.   Avoid the first double stroke.

Bass drum will be on beat 1 2 3 4.

Day 4 - Pattern - L**L** R L L R**R** L R R

Hand Pattern Applied to Drum Numbers Tempo = 54 (+8)

TIMING - EIGHTH NOTES - COUNTED AS 1 & 2 & 3 & 4 &

GUIDE

An example from the table - 3 4 1 2

Drum 3 (L**L** R L L) Drum 4 (R**R** L R R)
Drum 1 (L**L** R L L) Drum 2 (R**R** L R R)

Add the bass drum on each quarter note.

THIS IS A 2 BAR PATTERN

301

Hand Drum Numbers			
1234	2341	3412	4123
1243	2314	3421	4132
1324	2134	3124	4213
1342	2143	3142	4231
1423	2413	3214	4312
1432	2431	3241	4321

Day 5 - Pattern - LL R L L RR L R R

Hand Accents Applied to Drum Numbers Tempo = 54 (+8)

<u>TIMING - EIGHTH NOTES - COUNTED AS 1 & 2 & 3 & 4 &</u>

<u>GUIDE</u>

The pattern LL R L L RR L R R is played on the hi-hat or any drum including snare drum. However, every accent to be played, should be played according to the drum numbers.

PLAY NOTES AS CLOSE TOGETHER AS POSSIBLE, BASS DRUM PLAYING ALL QUARTER NOTES.

<u>THIS IS A 2 BAR PATTERN</u>.

Hand Drum Numbers			
1234	2341	3412	4123
1243	2314	3421	4132
1324	2134	3124	4213
1342	2143	3142	4231
1423	2413	3214	4312
1432	2431	3241	4321

Day 6 - Pattern - L**L** R L L R**R** L R R

Pattern as a Beat Tempo = 54 (+8)

<u>TIMING - EIGHTH NOTES - COUNTED AS **1 & 2 & 3 & 4 &**</u>

<u>GUIDE</u>

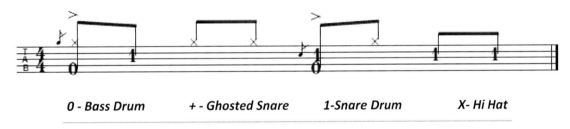

0 - Bass Drum   **+ - Ghosted Snare**   **1-Snare Drum**   **X- Hi Hat**

<u>ACCENTS ARE ON BEATS 1 AND 3</u>

Day 7 - Pattern - LL R L L RR L R R

Split Hand D. Numbers Tempo = 54 (+8)

<u>TIMING - EIGHTH NOTES - COUNTED AS 1 & 2 & 3 & 4 &</u>

<u>GUIDE</u>

Hand application, an example from the table - 3 4

Left hand remains on the first number **(3)**, whilst Right hand remains on the second number **(4)**.

<u>BASS DRUM SHOULD HAVE STEADY QUARTER NOTE PULSE.</u>

Drum Numbers			
12	23	32	41
13	24	34	42
14	21	31	43
1X	2X	3X	4X

304

Objective - Swiss Army Triplet - Right Lead

Swiss army triplet is based on a flam followed by a tap and another tap with the opposite limb. This is similar to a flam accent. Swiss army triplet can be used as an ideal replacement since repeated flam accents will have three taps on the same hand in a row, where as the Swiss army triplets only involve two taps on the same hand

CONSIDER THE DYNAMIC LEVELS AS **6** FOR THE ACCENT AND **3** FOR THE UNACCENTED, WITH NO OTHER CHANGE IN VOLUME.

The pattern is l**R** RL

305

Beat of the Week

The drum beat will support all exercises this week. Always use a metronome at the set tempo. Keep an eye on both hands and feet while practicing to develop better technique and effective posture.

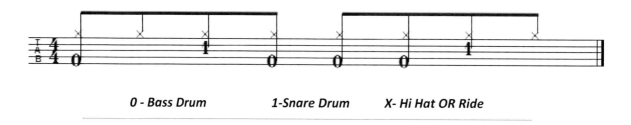

0 - Bass Drum   **1-Snare Drum**   **X- Hi Hat OR Ride**

Day 1 - Pattern - L **R** R L

Eighth Note Triplet Hand Tempo = 54 (+8)

TIMING - EIGHTH NOTES TRIPLET - COUNTED AS 1 TRIP LET 2 TRIP LET 3 TRIP LET 4 TRIP LET

<u>GUIDE</u>

Eighth Note triplet Count											
1	Trip	Let	**2**	Trip	Let	**3**	Trip	Let	**4**	Trip	Let
I**R**	R	L	I**R**	R	L	I**R**	R	L	I**R**	R	L

Maintain ACCENT is on each quarter note as a Flam.

Day 2 - Pattern - L **R** R L

Eighth Note Triplet Feet Tempo = 44 (+8)

TIMING - EIGHTH NOTES TRIPLET - COUNTED AS 1 TRIP LET 2 TRIP LET 3 TRIP LET 4 TRIP LET

GUIDE

Eighth Note triplet Count											
1	Trip	Let	**2**	Trip	Let	**3**	Trip	Let	**4**	Trip	Let
l**R**	R	L	l**R**	R	L	l**R**	R	L	l**R**	R	L

Maintain ACCENT is on each quarter note as a Flam.

Day 3 - Pattern - L **R** R L

Pattern as a Beat Tempo = 54 (+8)

TIMING - EIGHTH NOTES TRIPLET - COUNTED AS 1 TRIP LET 2 TRIP LET 3 TRIP LET 4 TRIP LET

GUIDE

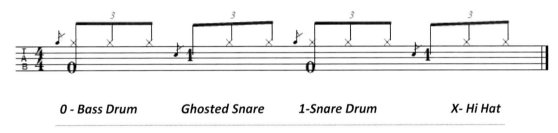

0 - Bass Drum   **Ghosted Snare**   **1-Snare Drum**   **X- Hi Hat**

ACCENT IS ON EACH QUARTER NOTE

Day 4 - Pattern - L **R** R L

Hand Pattern Applied to Drum Numbers Tempo = 54 (+8)

TIMING - EIGHTH NOTES TRIPLET - COUNTED AS **1** TRIP LET **2** TRIP LET **3** TRIP LET **4** TRIP LET

GUIDE

An example from the table - 3 4 1 2

Drum 3 (L**R** R L) Drum 4 (L**R** R L) Drum 1 (L**R** R L) Drum 2 (L**R** R L)

Add the bass drum on each quarter note.

THIS IS A **1** BAR PATTERN

Hand Drum Numbers			
1234	2341	3412	4123
1243	2314	3421	4132
1324	2134	3124	4213
1342	2143	3142	4231
1423	2413	3214	4312
1432	2431	3241	4321

Day 5 - Pattern - L **R** R L

Sixteenth Note Triplet Hand Tempo = 54 (+8)

TIMING - SIXTEENTH NOTES TRIPLET - COUNTED AS - 1 TRIP LET AND TRIP LET 2 TRIP LET AND TRIP LET 3 TRIP LET AND TRIP LET 4 TRIP LET AND TRIP LET

GUIDE

Sixteenth Note triplet Count																							
1	T	L	**&**	T	L	2	T	L	**&**	T	L	3	T	L	**&**	T	L	4	T	L	**&**	T	L
LR	R	L	LR	R	L	LR	R	L	LR	R	L	LR	R	L	LR	R	L	LR	R	L	LR	R	L

ACCENTS ARE IN BOLD ON EIGHTH NOTES.

Day 6 - Pattern - L **R** R L

Sixteenth Note Triplet Feet Tempo = 34 (+8)

<u>Timing - Sixteenth Notes Triplet - Counted as - 1 Trip Let and Trip Let 2 Trip Let and Trip Let 3 Trip Let and Trip Let 4 Trip Let and Trip Let</u>

<u>Guide</u>

Sixteenth Note triplet Count																							
1	T	L	&	T	L	2	T	L	&	T	L	3	T	L	&	T	L	4	T	L	&	T	L
LR	R	L	LR	R	L	LR	R	L	LR	R	L	LR	R	L	LR	R	L	LR	R	L	LR	R	L

<u>Accents are in bold</u>

Day 7 - Pattern - L **R** R L

Six Eight Note Hand or Feet Tempo = 46 (+8)

TIMING - SIX EIGHT NOTES - COUNTED AS 1 2 3 4 5 6

GUIDE

Six Eight Note Count Applied					
1	2	3	**4**	5	6
L**R**	R	L	L**R**	R	L

ACCENTS ARE IN BOLD ON BEATS **1** AND **4.**

Objective - Double Drag Tap - Left Lead

Double drag tap is a single drag tap with another grace note added before it. This is an alternating rudiment.

CONSIDER THE DYNAMIC LEVELS AS 6 FOR THE ACCENT AND 3 FOR THE UNACCENTED, WITH NO OTHER CHANGE IN VOLUME.

The pattern is rrL rrL **R** llR llR **L**

314

Beat of the Week

The drum beat will support all exercises this week. Always use a metronome at the set tempo. Keep an eye on both hands and feet while practicing to develop better technique and effective posture.

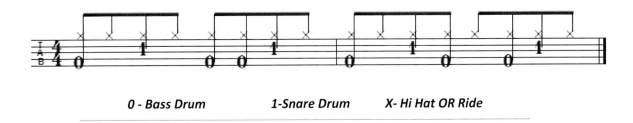

0 - Bass Drum   **1-Snare Drum**   **X- Hi Hat OR Ride**

Day 1 - Pattern - RRL RRL **R** LLR LLR **L**

Six Eighth Note Hand Tempo = 54 (+8)

<u>TIMING - SIX EIGHT NOTES - COUNTED AS **1 2 3 4 5 6**</u>

<u>GUIDE</u>

SIX Eight Note Count Applied					
1	2	**3**	4	5	**6**
RR L	RR L	**R**	LL R	LL R	**L**

Maintain ACCENT is on beats 3 and 6.

Day 2 - Pattern - RRL RRL **R** LLR LLR **L**

Six Eighth Feet Tempo = 46 (+8)

<u>TIMING - SIX EIGHT NOTES - COUNTED AS **1 2 3 4 5 6**</u>

<u>GUIDE</u>

SIX Eight Note Count Applied					
1	2	**3**	4	5	**6**
RR L	RR L	**R**	LL R	LL R	**L**

Maintain ACCENT is on beats 3 and 6.

Day 3 - Pattern - RRL RRL **R** LLR LLR **L**

Split Hand D. Numbers Tempo = 54 (+8)

TIMING - SIX EIGHT NOTES - COUNTED AS 1 2 3 4 5 6

GUIDE

Hand application, an example from the table - 3 4

Left hand remains on the first number **(3)**, whilst Right hand remains on the second number **(4)**.

BASS DRUM SHOULD BE ON BEATS 1 AND 4.

Drum Numbers			
12	23	32	41
13	24	34	42
14	21	31	43
1X	2X	3X	4X

Day 4 - Pattern - RRL RRL **R** LLR LLR **L**

Full Pattern Applied to Drum Numbers Accent on Snare Tempo = 54 (+8)

TIMING - SIX EIGHT NOTES - COUNTED AS 1 2 3 4 5 6

GUIDE

Hand application, an example from the table - 3 2 1 -
Drum 3 (2 Drags), Drum 1 (**Accent**),
Drum 2 (2 Drags) Drum 1 (**Accent**)

Drum 3 (RRL RRL), Drum 1 (**R**),
Drum 2 (LRR LLR), Drum 1 (**L**)

THIS IS A **1** BAR PATTERN

3 Hand Drum Numbers						
111	211	311	411	R11	X11	C11
121	221	321	421	R21	X21	C21
131	231	331	431	R31	X31	C31
141	241	341	441	R41	X41	C41
1R1	2R1	3R1	4R1	RR1	XR1	CR1
1X1	2X1	3X1	4X1	RX1	XX1	CX1

Day 5 - Pattern - RRL RRL **R** LLR LLR **L**

Hand Pattern Applied to Drum Numbers Tempo = 54 (+8)

TIMING - SIX EIGHT NOTES - COUNTED AS **1 2 3 4 5 6**

GUIDE

An example from the table - 3 4 1 2

Drum 3 (RRL RRL**)** Drum 4 (**R)** Drum 1 (LLR LLR**)** Drum 2 (**L)**

Add the bass drum to beats 1 and 4.

THIS IS A **1** BAR PATTERN

Hand Drum Numbers			
1234	2341	3412	4123
1243	2314	3421	4132
1324	2134	3124	4213
1342	2143	3142	4231
1423	2413	3214	4312
1432	2431	3241	4321

320

Day 6 - Pattern - RRL RRL **R** LLR LLR **L**

Split Hand+Foot D.Numbers Tempo = 54 (+8)

TIMING - SIX EIGHT NOTES - COUNTED AS 1 2 3 4 5 6

GUIDE

Application,

The first number / letter will be playing represents the L part of the rudiment, whilst the second number / letter will be playing represents the R part of the rudiment.

EXAMPLE LH - Y

LH (RR) Y (L)

Drum Numbers			
Split Limbs		**Abbreviation Guide**	
O	LH	0	Bass Drum
RH	O	RH	Right Hand
Y	RH	Y	Left Foot
LH	Y	LH	Left Hand
O	RH		
RH	Y		
Y	LH		
LH	O		

Day 7 - Pattern - RRL RRL **R** LLR LLR **L**

Split Hand+Foot D.Numbers Tempo = 54 (+8)

TIMING - SIX EIGHT NOTES - COUNTED AS 1 2 3 4 5 6

GUIDE

Application,

The first number / letter will be playing represents the L part of
the rudiment, whilst the second number / letter will be playing
represents the R part of the rudiment. The third number
represents the snare where the accent will be.

Drum Numbers			
Left Hand		Right Hand	
011	101	101	011
021	201	201	021
031	301	301	031
041	401	401	041
0X1	X01	X01	0X1
Y11	1Y1	1Y1	Y11
Y21	2Y1	2Y1	Y21
Y31	3Y1	3Y1	Y31
Y41	4Y1	4Y1	Y41
YX1	XY1	XY1	YX1

Objective - 6 Stroke Roll - Left Lead

Six stroke roll starts with an accented single note, followed by two doubles/diddles then another accented note.

CONSIDER THE DYNAMIC LEVELS AS 6 FOR THE ACCENT AND 3 FOR THE UNACCENTED, WITH NO OTHER CHANGE IN VOLUME.

The pattern is **L**RRLL**R**

323

Beat of the Week

The drum beat will support all exercises this week. Always use a metronome at the set tempo. Keep an eye on both hands and feet while practicing to develop better technique and effective posture.

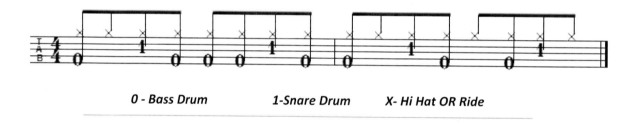

0 - Bass Drum   *1-Snare Drum*   *X- Hi Hat OR Ride*

Day 1 - Pattern - **L** R R L L **R**

Sixteenth Note Hand Tempo = 54 (+8)

TIMING - SIXTEENTH NOTES - COUNTED AS 1E &D 2 E & D 3 E & D 4 E & D

GUIDE

Sixteenth Note Count Applied															
1	E	&	**D**	**2**	E	&	**D**	**3**	E	&	**D**	**4**	E	&	**D**
L	RR	LL	**R**	**L**	RR	LL	**R**	**L**	RR	LL	**R**	**L**	RR	LL	**R**

Maintain ACCENTS on beats 3 and 6.

Day 2 - Pattern - **L** R R L L **R**

Sixteenth Note Feet Tempo = 34 (+8)

TIMING - SIXTEENTH NOTES - COUNTED AS 1E &D 2 E & D 3 E & D 4 E & D

GUIDE

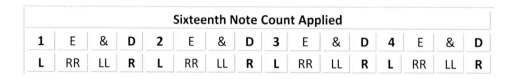

Sixteenth Note Count Applied															
1	E	&	**D**	**2**	E	&	**D**	**3**	E	&	**D**	**4**	E	&	**D**
L	RR	LL	**R**	**L**	RR	LL	**R**	**L**	RR	LL	**R**	**L**	RR	LL	**R**

Maintain ACCENT is on beats 3 and 6.

Day 3 - Pattern - **L** R R L L **R**

Split Hand D.Numbers Tempo = 54 (+8)
TIMING - SIXTEENTH NOTES - COUNTED AS 1E &D 2 E & D 3 E & D 4 E & D

GUIDE

Hand application, an example from the table - 3 4

Left hand remains on the first number **(3)**, whilst Right hand remains on the second number **(4)**.

BASS DRUM SHOULD BE ON BEATS 1 2 3 4.

Drum Numbers			
12	23	32	41
13	24	34	42
14	21	31	43
1X	2X	3X	4X

Day 4 - Pattern - **L** R R L L **R**

Hand Accents Applied to Drum Numbers Tempo = 54 (+8)

TIMING - SIXTEENTH NOTES - COUNTED AS 1E &D 2 E & D 3 E & D 4 E & D

GUIDE

The pattern **L** R R L L **R** is played on the hi-hat or any drum including snare drum. However, every accent to be played, should be played according to the drum numbers.

Left hand remains on the first number **(3)**, whilst Right hand remains on the second number **(4)**.

THIS IS A **1** BAR PATTERN. PLAY NOTES AS CLOSE TOGETHER AS POSSIBLE, BASS DRUM PLAYING ALL QUARTER NOTES.

Drum Numbers			
12	23	32	41
13	24	34	42
14	21	31	43
1X	2X	3X	4X

Day 5 - Pattern - **L** R R L L **R**

Hand Pattern Applied to DN, Accent On Snare Tempo = 54 (+8)

TIMING - SIXTEENTH NOTES - COUNTED AS 1E &D 2 E & D 3 E & D 4 E & D

GUIDE

The aim of this exercise is to play the accents only on the snare drum. The unaccented notes will follow the sequence of doubles according to the drum numbers.

4321 = SNARE **(L)**, 4 (RRLL) SNARE **(RL)** 3(RRLL) SNARE **(RL)**
DRUM 2 (RRLL) SNARE **(RL)** 1(RRLL) SNARE **(R)**

THIS IS A 1 BAR PATTERN

Hand Drum Numbers			
1234	2341	3412	4123
1243	2314	3421	4132
1324	2134	3124	4213
1342	2143	3142	4231
1423	2413	3214	4312
1432	2431	3241	4321

329

Day 6 - Pattern - **L** R R L L **R**

Cymbal Accents Applied to Drum Numbers Tempo = 54 (+8)
TIMING - SIXTEENTH NOTES - COUNTED AS 1E &D 2 E & D 3 E & D 4 E & D

GUIDE

The pattern starts with the **L** accent on the crash followed by R R L L
on the first number, **LR** on the crash, R R L L on **second number and
so on** is played according to the drum numbers with accent on
cymbals.

Bass drum should have quarter notes on beats 1, 2,3, 4

THIS IS A **1** BAR PATTERN

Hand Drum Numbers			
1234	2341	3412	4123
1243	2314	3421	4132
1324	2134	3124	4213
1342	2143	3142	4231
1423	2413	3214	4312
1432	2431	3241	4321

Day 7 - Pattern - **L** R R L L **R**

Split Hand + Foot D. Numbers Tempo = 54 (+8)
TIMING - SIXTEENTH NOTES - COUNTED AS 1E &D 2 E & D 3 E & D 4 E & D

GUIDE

Application,

The first number / letter will be playing represents the R part of the rudiment, whilst the second number / letter will be playing represents the L part of the rudiment.

EXAMPLE **LH - Y**

LH (L) Y (R)

Drum Numbers			
Split Limbs		**Abbreviation Guide**	
O	LH	0	Bass Drum
RH	O	RH	Right Hand
Y	RH	Y	Left Foot
LH	Y	LH	Left Hand
O	RH		
RH	Y		
Y	LH		
LH	O		

Objective - Lesson 25 - Right Lead

Lesson twenty five is three alternating notes with the first as drag, followed by single note and accented note with the opposite limb.

CONSIDER THE DYNAMIC LEVELS AS **6** FOR THE ACCENT AND **3** FOR THE UNACCENTED, WITH NO OTHER CHANGE IN VOLUME.

The pattern is llR L **R**

332

Beat of the Week

The drum beat will support all exercises this week. Always use a metronome at the set tempo. Keep an eye on both hands and feet while practicing to develop better technique and effective posture.

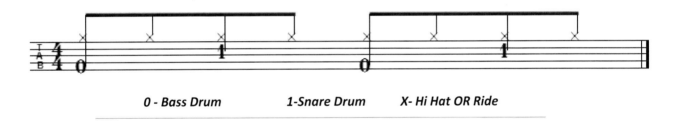

0 - Bass Drum   **1-Snare Drum**   **X- Hi Hat OR Ride**

Day 1 - Pattern - LLR L **R**

Sixteenth Note Hand Tempo = 54 (+8)

TIMING - SIXTEENTH NOTES - COUNTED AS 1E &D 2 E & D 3 E & D 4 E & D

GUIDE

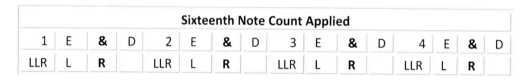

Sixteenth Note Count Applied															
1	E	**&**	D	2	E	**&**	D	3	E	**&**	D	4	E	**&**	D
LLR	L	**R**		LLR	L	**R**		LLR	L	**R**		LLR	L	**R**	

 ACCENT IS ON THE **AND** OF EACH QUARTER NOTE.

Day 2 - Pattern - LLR L **R**

Sixteenth Note Feet Tempo = 34 (+8)

TIMING - SIXTEENTH NOTES - COUNTED AS 1E &D 2 E & D 3 E & D 4 E & D

GUIDE

Sixteenth Note Count Applied															
1	E	**&**	D	2	E	**&**	D	3	E	**&**	D	4	E	**&**	D
LLR	L	**R**		LLR	L	**R**		LLR	L	**R**		LLR	L	**R**	

ACCENT IS ON THE **AND** OF EACH QUARTER NOTE.

Day 3 - Pattern - LLR L **R**

Full Hand Pattern Applied to Drum Numbers Tempo = 54 (+8)

TIMING - SIXTEENTH NOTES - COUNTED AS 1E &D 2 E & D 3 E & D 4 E & D

GUIDE

An example from the table - 3 4 1 2

Drum 3 (LLR L **R)** Drum 4 (LLR L **R)** Drum 1 (LLR L **R)** Drum 2 (LLR L **R)**

Add the bass drum on each quarter note.

THIS IS A **1** BAR PATTERN

Hand Drum Numbers			
1234	2341	3412	4123
1243	2314	3421	4132
1324	2134	3124	4213
1342	2143	3142	4231
1423	2413	3214	4312
1432	2431	3241	4321

Day 4 - Pattern - LLR L **R**

Hand Accents Applied to Drum Numbers Tempo = 54 (+8)

TIMING - SIXTEENTH NOTES - COUNTED AS 1E &D 2 E & D 3 E & D 4 E & D

GUIDE

The pattern LLR L **R** is played on the hi-hat or any drum including snare drum. However, every accent to be played, should be played according to the drum numbers.

PLAY NOTES AS CLOSE TOGETHER AS POSSIBLE, BASS DRUM PLAYING ALL QUARTER NOTES.

THIS IS A **1** BAR PATTERN.

337

Hand Drum Numbers			
1234	2341	3412	4123
1243	2314	3421	4132
1324	2134	3124	4213
1342	2143	3142	4231
1423	2413	3214	4312
1432	2431	3241	4321

Day 5 - Pattern - LLR L **R**

Pattern as a Beat Tempo = 54 (+8)

TIMING - SIXTEENTH NOTES - COUNTED AS 1E &D 2 E & D 3 E & D 4 E & D

GUIDE

0 - Bass Drum   *1-Snare Drum*   *X- Hi Hat*

ACCENT IS ON THE **AND** OF EACH QUARTER NOTE

Day 6 - Pattern - LLR L **R**

Pattern as a Beat Tempo = 54 (+8)

TIMING - SIXTEENTH NOTES - COUNTED AS 1E &D 2 E & D 3 E & D 4 E & D

GUIDE

0 - Bass Drum   *1-Snare Drum*   *X- Hi Hat*

ACCENT IS ON THE **AND** OF EACH QUARTER NOTE

Day 7 - Pattern - LLR L **R**

Split Hand Pattern Applied to Drum Numbers Tempo = 54 (+8)
TIMING - SIXTEENTH NOTES - COUNTED AS 1E &D 2 E & D 3 E & D 4 E & D

GUIDE

Hand application, an example from the table - 3 2 1 - Drum 3 (1 Drags), Drum 2 (Single), Drum 1 **(Accent)**

Drum 3 (LLR), Drum 2 (L), Drum 1 (**R**)

THIS IS A **1** BAR PATTERN

3 Hand Drum Numbers						
111	211	311	411	R11	X11	C11
121	221	321	421	R21	X21	C21
131	231	331	431	R31	X31	C31
141	241	341	441	R41	X41	C41
1R1	2R1	3R1	4R1	RR1	XR1	CR1
1X1	2X1	3X1	4X1	RX1	XX1	CX1

Objective - Double Paradiddle - Left Lead

Double paradiddle is a paradiddle with two singles before it, making double paradiddle a rudiment with 4 singles followed by a double/diddle. This is an alternating rudiment.

CONSIDER THE DYNAMIC LEVELS AS **6** FOR THE ACCENT AND **3** FOR THE UNACCENTED, WITH NO OTHER CHANGE IN VOLUME.

The pattern is **L** R L R L L **R** L R L R R

Beat of the Week

The drum beat will support all exercises this week. Always use a metronome at the set tempo. Keep an eye on both hands and feet while practicing to develop better technique and effective posture.

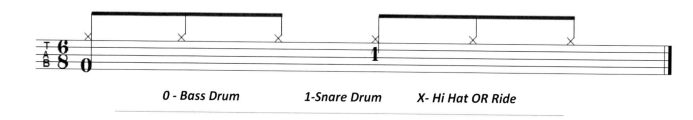

0 - Bass Drum   1-Snare Drum   X- Hi Hat OR Ride

Day 1 - Pattern - **L** R L R L L **R** L R L R R

Six Eighth Note Hand Tempo = 54 (+8)

TIMING - SIX EIGHT NOTES - COUNTED AS **1 2 3 4 5 6**

GUIDE

Six Eight Note Count Applied					
1	2	3	4	5	6
L	R	L	R	L	L
R	L	R	L	R	R

ACCENT IS ON BEAT **1**

Day 2 - Pattern - **L** R L R L L **R** L R L R R

Six Eighth Note Feet Tempo = 54 (+8)

TIMING - SIX EIGHT NOTES - COUNTED AS 1 2 3 4 5 6

GUIDE

Six Eight Note Count Applied					
1	2	3	4	5	6
L	R	L	R	L	L
R	L	R	L	R	R

ACCENT IS ON BEAT 1

Day 3 - Pattern - **L** R L R L L **R** L R L R R

Hand Pattern Applied to Drum Numbers Tempo = 54 (+8)

TIMING - SIX EIGHT NOTES - COUNTED AS 1 2 3 4 5 6

GUIDE

Hand application, an example from the table - 3 4

Left hand remains on the first number **(3)**, whilst Right hand remains on the second number **(4)**.

THIS IS A **2** BAR PATTERN

Drum Numbers			
12	23	32	41
13	24	34	42
14	21	31	43
1X	2X	3X	4X

Day 4 - Pattern - **L** R L R L L **R** L R L R R

Six Eighth Note Hand Tempo = 54 (+8)

<u>TIMING - SIX EIGHT NOTES - COUNTED AS **1 2 3 4 5 6**</u>

<u>GUIDE</u>

Six Eight Note Count Applied					
1	2	3	**4**	5	6
L R	L R	L L	**R** L	R L	R R

<u>ACCENT IS ON BEAT 1</u> .

Day 5 - Pattern - **L** R L R L L **R** L R L R R

Six Eighths Note Feet Tempo = 44 (+8)

<u>TIMING - SIX EIGHT NOTES - COUNTED AS **1 2 3 4 5 6**</u>

<u>GUIDE</u>

Six Eight Note Count Applied					
1	2	3	**4**	5	6
L R	L R	L L	**R** L	R L	R R

<u>ACCENT IS ON BEAT</u> 1 .

Day 6 - Pattern - **L** R L R L L **R** L R L R R

Split Pattern Applied to Drum Numbers Tempo = 54 (+8)

TIMING - SIX EIGHT NOTES - COUNTED AS 1 2 3 4 5 6

GUIDE

An example from the table - 3 4   1 2

Drum 3 (**L**RLR) Drum 4 (LL) Drum 1 (**R**LRL) Drum 2 (RR)

Add the bass drum to beats 1 and 4.

THIS IS A **1** BAR PATTERN

Hand Drum Numbers			
1234	2341	3412	4123
1243	2314	3421	4132
1324	2134	3124	4213
1342	2143	3142	4231
1423	2413	3214	4312
1432	2431	3241	4321

Day 7 - Pattern - **L** R L R L L **R** L R L R R

Split Hand Pattern Applied to DN, Accent On Snare Tempo = 54 (+8)

TIMING - SIX EIGHT NOTES - COUNTED AS **1 2 3 4 5 6**

GUIDE

The aim of this exercise is to play the accents only on the Snare drum. The unaccented notes will follow the sequence of doubles according to the drum numbers.

4321 = SNARE **(L)**, DRUM 4 (RLR) DRUM 3 (LL)
SNARE **(R)** DRUM 2 (LRL) DRUM 1 (RR)

THIS IS A 1 BAR PATTERN

Hand Drum Numbers			
1234	2341	3412	4123
1243	2314	3421	4132
1324	2134	3124	4213
1342	2143	3142	4231
1423	2413	3214	4312
1432	2431	3241	4321

Objective - Drag Paradiddle #1 Right Lead

Drag paradiddle #1 has the first note accented, followed by a paradiddle with drag grace notes on the first notes. This is an alternating rudiment.

CONSIDER THE DYNAMIC LEVELS AS 6 FOR THE ACCENT AND 3 FOR THE UNACCENTED, WITH NO OTHER CHANGE IN VOLUME.

The pattern is **R** llR L R R **L** rrL R L L

Beat of the Week

The drum beat will support all exercises this week. Always use a metronome at the set tempo. Keep an eye on both hands and feet while practicing to develop better technique and effective posture.

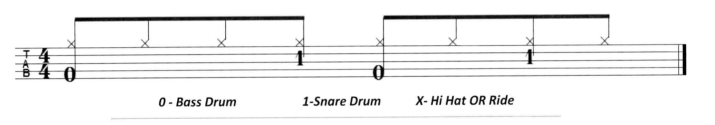

0 - Bass Drum   *1-Snare Drum*   *X- Hi Hat OR Ride*

Day 1 - Pattern - **R** LLR L R R **L** RRL R L L

Eighth Note Triplet Hand Tempo = 54 (+8)

TIMING - EIGHTH NOTES TRIPLET - COUNTED AS 1 TRIP LET 2 TRIP LET 3 TRIP LET 4 TRIP LET

GUIDE

Eighth Note triplet Count											
1	Trip	Let	2	Trip	Let	**3**	Trip	Let	4	Trip	Let
R		llR	L	R	R	**L**		rrL	R	L	L

ACCENT IS ON BEAT 1 AND 3

Day 2 - Pattern - **R** LLR L R R **L** RRL R L L

Eighth Note Triplet Feet Tempo = 48 (+8)

<u>TIMING - EIGHTH NOTES TRIPLET - COUNTED AS 1 TRIP LET 2 TRIP LET 3 TRIP LET 4 TRIP LET</u>

<u>GUIDE</u>

Eighth Note triplet Count											
1	Trip	Let	2	Trip	Let	3	Trip	Let	4	Trip	Let
R		llR	L	R	R	L		rrL	R	L	L

<u>ACCENT IS ON BEAT 1 AND 3</u>

353

Day 3 - Pattern - **R** LLR L R R **L** RRL R L L

Split Hand Pattern Applied to Drum Numbers Tempo = 54 (+8)

TIMING - EIGHTH NOTES TRIPLET - COUNTED AS 1 TRIP LET 2 TRIP LET 3 TRIP LET 4 TRIP LET

GUIDE

An example from the table - 3 4 1 2

Drum 3 (**R** LLR) Drum 4 (LRR) Drum 1 (L RRL) Drum 2 (RLL)

Add the bass drum to each quarter note - 1 2 3 4.

THIS IS A **1** BAR PATTERN

Hand Drum Numbers			
1234	2341	3412	4123
1243	2314	3421	4132
1324	2134	3124	4213
1342	2143	3142	4231
1423	2413	3214	4312
1432	2431	3241	4321

Day 4 - Pattern - **R** LLR L R R **L** RRL R L L

Split Hand Pattern Applied to Drum Numbers Tempo = 54 (+8)

TIMING - EIGHTH NOTES TRIPLET - COUNTED AS 1 TRIP LET 2 TRIP LET 3 TRIP LET 4 TRIP LET

GUIDE

Hand application, an example from the table - 3 4

Left hand remains on the first number **(3)**, whilst Right hand remains on the second number **(4)**.

THIS IS A **1** BAR PATTERN

Drum Numbers			
12	23	32	41
13	24	34	42
14	21	31	43
1X	2X	3X	4X

Day 5 - Pattern - **R** LLR L R R **L** RRL R L L

Split Hand + Foot D. Numbers Tempo = 54 (+8)

TIMING - EIGHTH NOTES TRIPLET - COUNTED AS 1 TRIP LET 2 TRIP LET 3 TRIP LET 4 TRIP LET

GUIDE

 Application,

The first number / letter will be playing represents the R part of the rudiment, whilst the second number / letter will be playing represents the L part of the rudiment.

EXAMPLE LH - Y

LH (L) Y (R)

Drum Numbers			
Split Limbs		**Abbreviation Guide**	
O	LH	0	Bass Drum
RH	O	RH	Right Hand
Y	RH	Y	Left Foot
LH	Y	LH	Left Hand
O	RH		
RH	Y		
Y	LH		
LH	O		

Day 6- Pattern- **R** LLR L R R **L** RRL R L L

Cymbal Tempo = 54 (+8)

TIMING - EIGHTH NOTES TRIPLET - COUNTED AS 1 TRIP LET 2 TRIP LET 3 TRIP LET 4 TRIP LET

GUIDE

Play the drag paradiddle pattern on one crash cymbal or multiple cymbals, maintaining accent on beats 1 and 3.

The pattern can be played as normal for multiple bars to build ambience in a ballad song.

Try the pattern with and without the bass drum for a variation of effects.

Day 7 - Pattern- **R** LLR L R R **L** RRL R L L

Hi-Hat Hand Tempo = 54 (+8)

TIMING - EIGHTH NOTES TRIPLET - COUNTED AS **1** TRIP LET **2** TRIP LET **3** TRIP LET **4** TRIP LET

GUIDE

Play the drag paradiddle pattern on the hi-hat firmly closed, whilst playing steady quarter notes on the bass drum. Start slow making sure the accents are correctly placed.

Bass drum will be on beat 1 2 3 4.

Objective - Inverted Flam Tap - Left Lead

Inverted flam tap has alternating diddles (offset by one sixteenth note) with a flam on the second note of each diddle. Also known as a tap flam. This is an alternating pattern within itself.

<u>CONSIDER THE DYNAMIC LEVELS AS **6** FOR THE ACCENT AND **3** FOR THE UNACCENTED, WITH NO OTHER CHANGE IN VOLUME.</u>

The pattern is r**L** R l**R** L

Beat of the Week

The drum beat will support all exercises this week. Always use a metronome at the set tempo. Keep an eye on both hands and feet while practicing to develop better technique and effective posture.

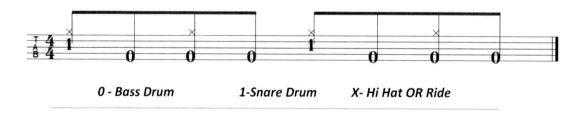

0 - Bass Drum   **1-Snare Drum**   **X- Hi Hat OR Ride**

Day 1 - Pattern - R**L** R L**R** L

Sixteenth Note Hand Tempo = 54 (+8)

<u>TIMING - SIXTEENTH NOTES - COUNTED AS 1E &D 2 E & D 3 E & D 4 E & D</u>

<u>GUIDE</u>

Sixteenth Note Count Applied															
1	E	**&**	D	**2**	E	**&**	D	**3**	E	**&**	D	**4**	E	**&**	D
RL	R	LR	L	RL	R	LR	L	RL	R	LR	L	RL	R	LR	L

<u>ACCENT IS ON ALL EIGHTH NOTES - 1 AND 2 AND 3 AND 4 AND</u>

Day 2 - Pattern - R**L** R L**R** L

Sixteenth Note Feet Tempo = 46 (+8)

TIMING - SIXTEENTH NOTES - COUNTED AS 1E &D 2 E & D 3 E & D 4 E & D

GUIDE

ACCENT IS ON ALL EIGHTH NOTES - 1 AND 2 AND 3 AND 4 AND

Day 3 - Pattern - R**L** R L**R** L

Full Hand Pattern Applied to Drum Numbers Tempo = 54 (+8)

TIMING - SIXTEENTH NOTES - COUNTED AS 1E &D 2 E & D 3 E & D 4 E & D

GUIDE

Quarter note value per drum

An example from the table - 3 4 1 2

Drum 3 (R**L** R L**R** L) Drum 4 (R**L** R L**R** L)
Drum 1 (R**L** R L**R** L) Drum 2 (R**L** R L**R** L)

THIS IS A **1** BAR PATTERN

Hand Drum Numbers			
1234	2341	3412	4123
1243	2314	3421	4132
1324	2134	3124	4213
1342	2143	3142	4231
1423	2413	3214	4312
1432	2431	3241	4321

Day 4 - Pattern - R**L** R L**R** L

Split Hand Pattern Applied to Drum Numbers Tempo = 54 (+8)

Timing - Sixteenth Notes - Counted as 1 e &d 2 e & d 3 e & d 4 e & d

Guide

Eighth note value per drum

An example from the table - 3 4 1 2

Drum 3 (R**L** R) Drum 4 (L**R** L) Drum 1 (R**L** R) Drum 2 (L**R** L)

This is a 1 bar pattern, however the pattern is executed twice within the bar.

Hand Drum Numbers			
1234	2341	3412	4123
1243	2314	3421	4132
1324	2134	3124	4213
1342	2143	3142	4231
1423	2413	3214	4312
1432	2431	3241	4321

Day 5 - Pattern - R**L** R L**R** L

Hand Pattern Applied to Drum Numbers Tempo = 54 (+8)

TIMING - SIXTEENTH NOTES - COUNTED AS 1E &D 2 E & D 3 E & D 4 E & D

GUIDE

Sixteenth note value per drum

An example from the table - 3 4 1 2

Drum 3 (R**L**) Drum 4 (R) Drum 1 (L**R**) Drum 2 (L)

THIS IS A **1** BAR PATTERN, HOWEVER THE PATTERN IS EXECUTED **4** TIMES WITHIN THE BAR.

Hand Drum Numbers			
1234	2341	3412	4123
1243	2314	3421	4132
1324	2134	3124	4213
1342	2143	3142	4231
1423	2413	3214	4312
1432	2431	3241	4321

Day 6- Pattern- R**L** R L**R** L

Hi-Hat Hand Tempo = 54 (+8)

TIMING - SIXTEENTH NOTES - COUNTED AS 1E &D 2 E & D 3 E & D 4 E & D

GUIDE

Play the Inverted flam tap pattern on the hi-hat firmly closed, whilst playing steady quarter notes on the bass drum. Start slow making sure the accents are correctly placed.

Bass drum will be on beat 1 2 3 4.

Day 7 - Pattern - R**L** R L**R** L

Split Hand + Foot D. Numbers Tempo = 54 (+8)

TIMING - SIXTEENTH NOTES - COUNTED AS 1E &D 2 E & D 3 E & D 4 E & D

GUIDE

Application,

The first number / letter will be playing represents the R part of the rudiment, whilst the second number / letter will be playing represents the L part of the rudiment.

EXAMPLE LH - Y

LH (L) Y (R)

Drum Numbers			
Split Limbs		Abbreviation Guide	
O	LH	0	Bass Drum
RH	O	RH	Right Hand
Y	RH	Y	Left Foot
LH	Y	LH	Left Hand
O	RH		
RH	Y		
Y	LH		
LH	O		

Objective - 13 Stroke Roll - Right Lead

Thirteen stroke roll is 6 doubles followed by an accented note.

CONSIDER THE DYNAMIC LEVELS AS **6** FOR THE ACCENT AND **3** FOR THE UNACCENTED, WITH NO OTHER CHANGE IN VOLUME.

The pattern is RRLLRRLLRRLL**R**

Beat of the Week

The drum beat will support all exercises this week. Always use a metronome at the set tempo. Keep an eye on both hands and feet while practicing to develop better technique and effective posture.

0 - Bass Drum   **+ - Ghosted Snare**   **1-Snare Drum**   **X- Hi Hat**

Day 1 - Pattern - RRLL RRLL RRLL **R**

Sixteenth Note Hand Tempo = 54 (+8)

TIMING - SIXTEENTH NOTES - COUNTED AS 1E &D 2 E & D 3 E & D 4 E & D

GUIDE

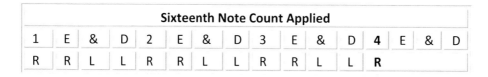

Sixteenth Note Count Applied															
1	E	&	D	2	E	&	D	3	E	&	D	**4**	E	&	D
R	R	L	L	R	R	L	L	R	R	L	L	**R**			

ACCENT IS ON BEAT 4

Day 2 - Pattern - RRLL RRLL RRLL **R**

Sixteenth Note Feet Tempo = 34 (+8)

<u>TIMING - SIXTEENTH NOTES - COUNTED AS 1E &D 2 E & D 3 E & D 4 E & D</u>

<u>GUIDE</u>

Sixteenth Note Count Applied															
1	E	&	D	2	E	&	D	3	E	&	D	**4**	E	&	D
R	R	L	L	R	R	L	L	R	R	L	L	**R**			

<u>ACCENT IS ON BEAT 4</u>

Day 3 - Pattern - RRLL RRLL RRLL **R**

Hand Pattern Applied to Drum Numbers Tempo = 54 (+8)

TIMING - SIXTEENTH NOTES - COUNTED AS 1E &D 2 E & D 3 E & D 4 E & D

GUIDE

Quarter note value per drum

An example from the table - 3 4 1 2

Drum 3 (RRLL) Drum 4 (RRLL) Drum 1 (RRLL) Drum 2 (**R**)

THIS IS A **2** BAR PATTERN

Hand Drum Numbers			
1234	2341	3412	4123
1243	2314	3421	4132
1324	2134	3124	4213
1342	2143	3142	4231
1423	2413	3214	4312
1432	2431	3241	4321

Day 4 - Pattern - RRLL RRLL RRLL **R**

Hand Pattern Applied to DN, Accent On Snare Tempo = 54 (+8)

<u>Timing - Sixteenth Notes - Counted as 1e &d 2 e & d 3 e & d 4 e & d</u>

<u>Guide</u>

The aim of this exercise is to play the accents only on the snare drum. The unaccented notes will follow the sequence of doubles according to the drum numbers.

432 = 4 (RRLL) 3(RRLL) 2 (RRLL) 1(R)

<u>This is a 1 bar pattern</u>

Hand Drum Numbers			
123	234	341	412
124	231	342	413
132	213	312	421
134	214	314	423
142	241	321	431
143	243	324	432

Day 5 - Pattern - RRLL RRLL RRLL **R**

Rotational Hand Pattern Applied to DN, Accent On Snare Tempo = 54 (+8)

<u>TIMING - SIXTEENTH NOTES - COUNTED AS 1E &D 2 E & D 3 E & D 4 E & D</u>

GUIDE

The aim of this exercise is to play the accents only on the snare drum. The unaccented notes will follow the sequence of doubles according to the drum numbers. Start on Beat 2. Accent always finishes on Beat 1

1234 = DRUM 1 (RRLL) DRUM 2 (RRLL) DRUM 3 (RRLL) DRUM 1(**R**)
FOLLOWED BY DRUM 2(RRLL) DRUM 3 (RRLL) DRUM 4 (RRLL) 1 (**R**)

<u>THIS IS A 2 BAR PATTERN</u>

Hand Drum Numbers			
1234	2341	3412	4123
1243	2314	3421	4132
1324	2134	3124	4213
1342	2143	3142	4231
1423	2413	3214	4312
1432	2431	3241	4321

374

Day 6 - Pattern - RRLL RRLL RRLL **R**

Split Hand + Feet D. Numbers Tempo = 54 (+8)

TIMING - SIXTEENTH NOTES - COUNTED AS 1E &D 2 E & D 3 E & D 4 E & D

GUIDE

The aim of this exercise is to play the accents only on the snare drum. The unaccented notes will follow the sequence of doubles according to the drum numbers from previous exercise. Start on beat 2 so accent always finishes on Beat 1.

THIS IS A 2 BAR PATTERN

Drum Numbers			
Split Limbs		Abbreviation Guide	
O	LH	0	Bass Drum
RH	O	RH	Right Hand
Y	RH	Y	Left Foot
LH	Y	LH	Left Hand
O	RH		
RH	Y		
Y	LH		
LH	O		

Day 7 - Pattern - RRLL RRLL RRLL **R**

Pattern as a Beat on Foot Tempo = 54 (+8)

<u>TIMING - SIXTEENTH NOTES - COUNTED AS 1E &D 2 E & D 3 E & D 4 E & D</u>

<u>GUIDE</u>

0 - Bass Drum   *1-Snare Drum*   *X- Hi Hat*

<u>ACCENT IS ON BEAT 4</u>

Objective - Triple Ratamacue - Left Lead

Triple Ratamacue is a single Ratamacue with 2 drags before it. This is an alternating rudiment.

CONSIDER THE DYNAMIC LEVELS AS **6** FOR THE ACCENT AND **3** FOR THE UNACCENTED, WITH NO OTHER CHANGE IN VOLUME.

The pattern is rrL rrL rrL R L **R**   llR llR llR L R **L**

Beat of the Week

The drum beat will support all exercises this week. Always use a metronome at the set tempo. Keep an eye on both hands and feet while practicing to develop better technique and effective posture.

0 - Bass Drum   *1-Snare Drum*   *X- Hi Hat*

Day 1 -Pattern-rrL rrL rrLRL**R** llR llR llRLR**L**

Sixteenth Note Triplet Hand Tempo = 54 (+8)

TIMING - SIXTEENTH NOTES TRIPLET - COUNTED AS - 1 TRIP LET AND TRIP LET 2 TRIP LET AND TRIP LET 3 TRIP LET AND TRIP LET 4 TRIP LET AND TRIP LET

GUIDE

Sixteenth Note triplet Count																							
1	T	L	&	T	L	2	T	L	**&**	T	L	3	T	L	&	T	L	4	T	L	**&**	T	L
rL		rrL		rrL	R	L	**R**			IIR			IIR			Llr	L	R	**L**				

ACCENTS ARE IN BOLD ON THE **AND** OF 2 AND 4.

Day 2 -Pattern-rrL rrL rrLRL**R** llR llR llRLR**L**

Sixteenth Note Triplet Feet Tempo = 54 (+8)

TIMING - SIXTEENTH NOTES TRIPLET - COUNTED AS - 1 TRIP LET AND TRIP LET 2 TRIP LET AND TRIP LET 3 TRIP LET AND TRIP LET 4 TRIP LET AND TRIP LET

GUIDE

Sixteenth Note triplet Count																							
1	T	L	&	T	L	2	T	L	**&**	T	L	3	T	L	&	T	L	4	T	L	**&**	T	L
rrL			rrL			rrL	R	L	**R**			llR			llR			Llr	L	R	**L**		

ACCENTS ARE IN BOLD

Day 3 -Pattern-rrL rrL rrLRL**R** llR llR llRLRL

Split Hand D. Numbers Tempo = 54 (+8)

TIMING - SIXTEENTH NOTES TRIPLET - COUNTED AS - 1 TRIP LET AND TRIP LET 2 TRIP LET AND TRIP LET 3 TRIP LET AND TRIP LET 4 TRIP LET AND TRIP LET

GUIDE

Hand application, an example from the table - 3 4

Left hand remains on the first number **(3)**, whilst Right hand remains on the second number **(4)**.

BASS DRUM SHOULD HAVE STEADY QUARTER NOTE PULSE.

Drum Numbers			
12	23	32	41
13	24	34	42
14	21	31	43
1X	2X	3X	4X

Day 4 -Pattern-rrL rrL rrLRL**R** llR llR llRLRL**L**

Hand + Feet D. Numbers Tempo = 44 (+8)

TIMING - SIXTEENTH NOTES TRIPLET - COUNTED AS - 1 TRIP LET AND TRIP LET 2 TRIP LET AND TRIP LET 3 TRIP LET AND TRIP LET 4 TRIP LET AND TRIP LET

GUIDE

BASS DRUM SHOULD PLAY STEADY QUARTER NOTES.

ONCE COMFORTABLE, APPLY TO THE HAND DRUM NUMBERS ACROSS THE KIT.

An example from the table - 3 4 1 2

Drum 3 (rrl rrl) Drum 4 (rrl R L **R**) Drum 1 (llr llr) Drum 2 (llr L R **L**)

Hand Drum Numbers			
1234	2341	3412	4123
1243	2314	3421	4132
1324	2134	3124	4213
1342	2143	3142	4231
1423	2413	3214	4312
1432	2431	3241	4321

Day 5 -Pattern-rrL rrL rrLRL**R** llR llR llRLRL**L**

Split Hand + Feet D. Numbers Tempo = 54 (+8)

TIMING - SIXTEENTH NOTES TRIPLET - COUNTED AS - 1 TRIP LET AND TRIP LET 2 TRIP LET AND TRIP LET 3 TRIP LET AND TRIP LET 4 TRIP LET AND TRIP LET

GUIDE

Application,

The first number / letter will be playing represents the R part of the rudiment, whilst the second number / letter will be playing represents the L part of the rudiment.

Drum Numbers			
Split Limbs		Abbreviation Guide	
O	LH	0	Bass Drum
RH	O	RH	Right Hand
Y	RH	Y	Left Foot
LH	Y	LH	Left Hand
O	RH		
RH	Y		
Y	LH		
LH	O		

Day 6 -Pattern-rrL rrL rrLRL**R** llR llR llRLR**L**

Hand Pattern Applied to DN, Accent On Snare Tempo = 54 (+8)

TIMING - SIXTEENTH NOTES TRIPLET - COUNTED AS - **1** TRIP LET AND TRIP LET **2** TRIP LET AND TRIP LET **3** TRIP LET AND TRIP LET **4** TRIP LET AND TRIP LET

GUIDE

The aim of this exercise is to play the accents only on the snare drum. The unaccented notes will follow the drum numbers according to day 4 . An example from the table - 3 4 1 2

Drum 3 (rrl rrl) Drum 4 (rrl R L) Drum 1 (**R**)
Drum 1 (llr llr) Drum 2 (llr L R) Drum 1 (**L**)

Maintain Accent always

Hand Drum Numbers			
1234	2341	3412	4123
1243	2314	3421	4132
1324	2134	3124	4213
1342	2143	3142	4231
1423	2413	3214	4312
1432	2431	3241	4321

Day 7 -Pattern-rrL rrL rrLRL**R** llR llR llRLR**L**

Hand Accents Applied to Drum Numbers Tempo = 54 (+8)

TIMING - SIXTEENTH NOTES TRIPLET - COUNTED AS - 1 TRIP LET AND TRIP LET 2 TRIP LET AND TRIP LET 3
TRIP LET AND TRIP LET 4 TRIP LET AND TRIP LET

GUIDE

The pattern rrL rrL rrLRL**R** llR llR llRLR**L** is played on the hi-hat or any drum of choice including Snare drum. However, every accent to be played, should be played according to the drum numbers.

PLAY NOTES AS CLOSE TOGETHER AS POSSIBLE, BASS DRUM PLAYING ALL QUARTER NOTES.

THIS IS A 2 BAR PATTERN.

Hand Drum Numbers			
1234	2341	3412	4123
1243	2314	3421	4132
1324	2134	3124	4213
1342	2143	3142	4231
1423	2413	3214	4312
1432	2431	3241	4321

Objective - Flamacue - Right Lead

Flamacue is a group of five notes, four being sixteenth notes and the fifth ends on the downbeat. The first note /down beat is a flam, and the second note is accented.

<u>**C**ONSIDER THE DYNAMIC LEVELS AS **6** FOR THE ACCENT AND **3** FOR THE UNACCENTED, WITH NO OTHER CHANGE IN VOLUME.</u>

The pattern is lR **L** R L R

Beat of the Week

The drum beat will support all exercises this week. Always use a metronome at the set tempo. Keep an eye on both hands and feet while practicing to develop better technique and effective posture.

0 - Bass Drum   1-Snare Drum   X- Hi Hat

Day 1 - Pattern - lR **L** R L lR

Sixteenth Note Hand Tempo = 54 (+8)

<u>TIMING - SIXTEENTH NOTES - COUNTED AS 1E &D 2 E & D 3 E & D 4 E & D</u>

<u>GUIDE</u>

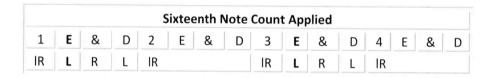

Sixteenth Note Count Applied															
1	**E**	&	D	2	E	&	D	3	**E**	&	D	4	E	&	D
lR	**L**	R	L	lR				lR	**L**	R	L	lR			

<u>ACCENT IS ON E OF SIXTEENTH COUNT OF 1 AND 3</u>

Day 2 - Pattern - lR **L** R L lR

Sixteenth Note Feet Tempo = 34 (+8)

TIMING - SIXTEENTH NOTES - COUNTED AS 1E &D 2 E & D 3 E & D 4 E & D

GUIDE

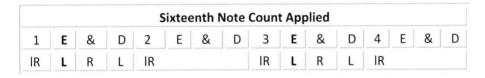

Sixteenth Note Count Applied															
1	E	&	D	2	E	&	D	3	E	&	D	4	E	&	D
lR	L	R	L	lR				lR	L	R	L	lR			

ACCENT IS ON E OF SIXTEENTH COUNT OF 1 AND 3

389

Day 3 - Pattern - lR **L** R L lR

Split Hand + Feet D. Numbers Tempo = 54 (+8)
TIMING - SIXTEENTH NOTES - COUNTED AS 1E &D 2 E & D 3 E & D 4 E & D

GUIDE

Application,

The first number / letter will be playing represents the R part of the rudiment, whilst the second number / letter will be playing represents the L part of the rudiment.

Drum Numbers			
Split Limbs		Abbreviation Guide	
O	LH	O	Bass Drum
RH	O	RH	Right Hand
Y	RH	Y	Left Foot
LH	Y	LH	Left Hand
O	RH		
RH	Y		
Y	LH		
LH	O		

Day 4 -Pattern- lR **L** R L lR

Split Hand D. Numbers Tempo = 54 (+8)

TIMING - SIXTEENTH NOTES - COUNTED AS 1E &D 2 E & D 3 E & D 4 E & D

GUIDE

Hand application, an example from the table - 3 4

Left hand remains on the first number **(3)**, whilst Right hand remains on the second number **(4)**.

BASS DRUM SHOULD HAVE STEADY QUARTER NOTE PULSE.

Drum Numbers			
12	23	32	41
13	24	34	42
14	21	31	43
1X	2X	3X	4X

Day 5 - Pattern - lR **L** R L lR

Hand Accents Applied to Drum Numbers Tempo = 54 (+8)

<u>TIMING - SIXTEENTH NOTES - COUNTED AS 1E &D 2 E & D 3 E & D 4 E & D</u>

<u>GUIDE</u>

The pattern lR L R **L** lR is played on the hi-hat or any drum of choice including snare drum. However, every accent to be played, should be played according to the drum numbers.

<u>THIS IS A **1** BAR PATTERN</u>.

<u>PLAY NOTES AS CLOSE TOGETHER AS POSSIBLE, IN TIME</u>.

Drum Numbers			
12	23	32	41
13	24	34	42
14	21	31	43
1X	2X	3X	4X

Day 6- Pattern- lR **L** R L lR

Cymbal Tempo = 54 (+8)

TIMING - SIXTEENTH NOTES - COUNTED AS 1E &D 2 E & D 3 E & D 4 E & D

GUIDE

Play the Flamacue pattern on one crash cymbal or multiple cymbals, maintaining the accent on the 'E' of the 16th note of beats 1 and 3.

The pattern can be played as normal for multiple bars to build ambience in a ballad song or at the end.

Try the pattern with and without the bass drum for a variation of effects.

Day 7- Pattern- lR **L** R L lR

Hi-Hat Hand Tempo = 54 (+8)

TIMING - SIXTEENTH NOTES - COUNTED AS 1E &D 2 E & D 3 E & D 4 E & D

GUIDE

Play the Flamacue pattern on the hi-hat firmly closed, whilst playing steady quarter notes on the bass drum. Start slow making sure the accents are correctly placed.

Bass drum will be on beat 1 2 3 4.

Once comfortable, move the accents onto the snare drum (1).

Objective - Inverted Double Stroke #1- Right

Inverted double stroke #1 for this week will be based on a triplet feel with the accent being on the first right note of the doubles, which happens to fall on the D of each quarter note.

CONSIDER THE DYNAMIC LEVELS AS **6** FOR THE ACCENT AND **3** FOR THE UNACCENTED, WITH NO OTHER CHANGE IN VOLUME.

The pattern is R L L **R** R L L **R** R L L **R**

Beat of the Week

The drum beat will support all exercises this week. Always use a metronome at the set tempo. Keep an eye on both hands and feet while practicing to develop better technique and effective posture.

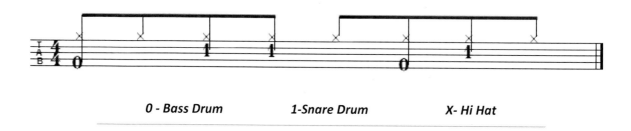

0 - Bass Drum   *1-Snare Drum*   *X- Hi Hat*

Day 1 - Pattern - RLL**R**

Sixteenth Note Hand Tempo = 54 (+8)

TIMING - SIXTEENTH NOTES - COUNTED AS 1E &D 2 E & D 3 E & D 4 E & D

GUIDE

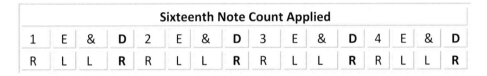

Sixteenth Note Count Applied															
1	E	&	**D**	2	E	&	**D**	3	E	&	**D**	4	E	&	**D**
R	L	L	**R**	R	L	L	**R**	R	L	L	**R**	R	L	L	**R**

ACCENT IS IN BOLD

Day 2 - Pattern - RLL**R**

Sixteenth Note Feet Tempo = 34 (+8)

GUIDE

Sixteenth Note Count Applied															
1	E	&	**D**	2	E	&	**D**	3	E	&	**D**	4	E	&	**D**
R	L	L	**R**	R	L	L	**R**	R	L	L	**R**	R	L	L	**R**

ACCENT IS IN BOLD.

Day 3 - Pattern - RLL**R**

Hand Pattern Applied to Drum Numbers Tempo = 54 (+8)

TIMING - SIXTEENTH NOTES - COUNTED AS 1E &D 2 E & D 3 E & D 4 E & D

GUIDE

Quarter note value per drum

An example from the table - 3 4 1 2

Drum 3 (RLL**R**) Drum 4 (RLL**R**) Drum 1 (RLL**R**) Drum 2 (RLL**R**)

THIS IS A **1** BAR PATTERN

Hand Drum Numbers			
1234	2341	3412	4123
1243	2314	3421	4132
1324	2134	3124	4213
1342	2143	3142	4231
1423	2413	3214	4312
1432	2431	3241	4321

Day 4 - Pattern - RLL**R**

Split Hand + Feet D. Numbers Tempo = 54 (+8)

TIMING - SIXTEENTH NOTES - COUNTED AS 1E &D 2 E & D 3 E & D 4 E & D

GUIDE

Application,

The first number / letter will be playing represents the R part of the rudiment, whilst the second number / letter will be playing represents the L part of the rudiment.

Drum Numbers			
Split Limbs		Abbreviation Guide	
O	LH	0	Bass Drum
RH	O	RH	Right Hand
Y	RH	Y	Left Foot
LH	Y	LH	Left Hand
O	RH		
RH	Y		
Y	LH		
LH	O		

Day 5 - Pattern - RLL**R**

Eighth Note Triplet Hand Tempo = 54 (+8)

TIMING - EIGHTH NOTE TRIPLET - COUNTED AS 1 TRIP LET 2 TRIP LET 3 TRIP LET 4 TRIP LET

GUIDE

Eighth Note triplet Count											
1	Trip	Let	**2**	Trip	Let	3	**Trip**	Let	4	Trip	**Let**
R	L	L	**R**	R	L	L	**R**	R	L	L	**R**

BASS DRUM SHOULD PLAY STEADY QUARTER NOTES

ONCE YOU ARE COMFORTABLE WITH THE EXERCISE, APPLY TO THE HAND DRUM NUMBERS ACROSS THE KIT AND APPLY AS A DRUM FILL.

ACCENT IS ON BEAT 2, TRIP OF 3 AND LET OF 4.

Day 6 - Pattern - RLL**R**

Eighth Note Triplet Feet Tempo = 48 (+8)

TIMING - EIGHTH NOTE TRIPLET - COUNTED AS 1 TRIP LET 2 TRIP LET 3 TRIP LET 4 TRIP LET

GUIDE

Eighth Note triplet Count											
1	Trip	Let	**2**	Trip	Let	3	**Trip**	Let	4	Trip	**Let**
R	L	L	**R**	R	L	L	**R**	R	L	L	**R**

ACCENT IS ON BEAT 2, TRIP OF 3 AND LET OF 4.

Day 7 - Pattern - RLL**R**

Hand Pattern Applied to Drum Numbers Tempo = 54 (+8)

TIMING - EIGHTH NOTE TRIPLET - COUNTED AS 1 TRIP LET 2 TRIP LET 3 TRIP LET 4 TRIP LET

GUIDE

Quarter note value per drum

An example from the table - 3 4 1 2

Drum 3 (RLL) Drum 4 (**R**RL) Drum 1 (L**R**R) Drum 2 (LL**R**)

THIS IS A **1** BAR PATTERN

Hand Drum Numbers			
1234	2341	3412	4123
1243	2314	3421	4132
1324	2134	3124	4213
1342	2143	3142	4231
1423	2413	3214	4312
1432	2431	3241	4321

Objective - 9 Stroke Roll - Left Lead

Nine stroke roll is 4 doubles / diddles followed by an accented note.

CONSIDER THE DYNAMIC LEVELS AS 6 FOR THE ACCENT AND 3 FOR THE UNACCENTED, WITH NO OTHER CHANGE IN VOLUME.

The pattern is L L R R L L R R **L**

Beat of the Week

The drum beat will support all exercises this week. Always use a metronome at the set tempo. Keep an eye on both hands and feet while practicing to develop better technique and effective posture.

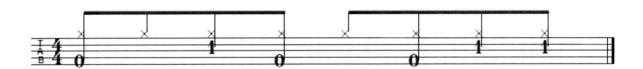

0 - Bass Drum   **1-Snare Drum**   **X- Hi Hat**

Day 1 - Pattern - LLRR LLRR **L**

Sixteenth Note Hand Tempo = 54 (+8)

TIMING - SIXTEENTH NOTES - COUNTED AS 1E &D 2 E & D 3 E & D 4 E & D

GUIDE

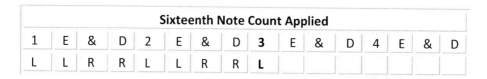

Sixteenth Note Count Applied															
1	E	&	D	2	E	&	D	**3**	E	&	D	4	E	&	D
L	L	R	R	L	L	R	R	**L**							

ACCENT IS ON BEAT 3.

Day 2 - Pattern - LLRR LLRR **L**

Sixteenth Note Feet Tempo = 38 (+8)

<u>TIMING - SIXTEENTH NOTES - COUNTED AS 1E &D 2 E & D 3 E & D 4 E & D</u>

<u>GUIDE</u>

Sixteenth Note Count Applied															
1	E	&	D	2	E	&	D	**3**	E	&	D	4	E	&	D
L	L	R	R	L	L	R	R	**L**							

<u>ACCENT IS ON BEAT 3.</u>

407

Day 3 - Pattern - LLRR LLRR **L**

Split Hand Pattern Applied to Drum Numbers Tempo = 54 (+8)

TIMING - SIXTEENTH NOTES - COUNTED AS 1E &D 2 E & D 3 E & D 4 E & D

GUIDE

Hand application, an example from the table - 3 2 1 -
Drum 3 (LLRR), Drum 2 (LLRR), Drum 1 (**L**)

THIS IS A **1** BAR PATTERN

3 Hand Drum Numbers						
111	211	311	411	R11	X11	C11
121	221	321	421	R21	X21	C21
131	231	331	431	R31	X31	C31
141	241	341	441	R41	X41	C41
1R1	2R1	3R1	4R1	RR1	XR1	CR1
1X1	2X1	3X1	4X1	RX1	XX1	CX1

Day 4 - Pattern - LLRR LLRR **L**

Split Hand + Feet D. Numbers Tempo = 34 (+8)

TIMING - SIXTEENTH NOTES - COUNTED AS 1E &D 2 E & D 3 E & D 4 E & D

GUIDE

Application,

The first number / letter will be playing represents the R part of the rudiment, whilst the second number / letter will be playing represents the L part of the rudiment.

Drum Numbers			
Split Limbs		Abbreviation Guide	
O	LH	0	Bass Drum
RH	O	RH	Right Hand
Y	RH	Y	Left Foot
LH	Y	LH	Left Hand
O	RH		
RH	Y		
Y	LH		
LH	O		

Day 5 - Pattern - LLRR LLRR **L**

Thirty Second Note Hand Tempo = 54 (+8)

TIMING -THIRTY-SECOND NOTES - COUNTED AS 1E &D & E &D 2 E &D & E &D 3 E &D & E &D 4 E &D & E &D

GUIDE

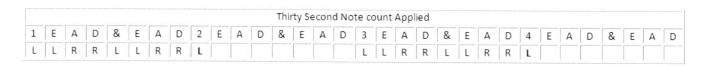

Thirty Second Note count Applied																															
1	E	A	D	&	E	A	D	2	E	A	D	&	E	A	D	3	E	A	D	&	E	A	D	4	E	A	D	&	E	A	D
L	L	R	R	L	L	R	R	**L**								L	L	R	R	L	L	R	R	**L**							

ACCENTS ARE IN BOLD

Day 6 - Pattern - LLRR LLRR **L**

Thirty Second Note Feet Tempo = 30 (+8)

TIMING -THIRTY-SECOND NOTES - COUNTED AS 1E &D & E &D 2 E &D & E &D 3 E &D & E &D 4 E &D & E &D

GUIDE

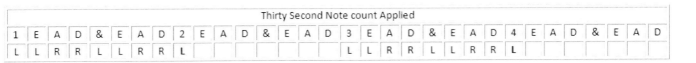

1	E	A	D	&	E	A	D	2	E	A	D	&	E	A	D	3	E	A	D	&	E	A	D	4	E	A	D	&	E	A	D
L	L	R	R	L	L	R	R	**L**								L	L	R	R	L	L	R	R	**L**							

ACCENTS ARE IN BOLD

411

Day 7 - Pattern - LLRR LLRR **L**

Hand Pattern Applied Rotational D. Numbers Tempo = 54 (+8)

Timing -Thirty-second Notes - Counted as 1e &d & e &d 2 e &d & e &d 3 e &d & e &d 4 e &d & e &d

Guide

Quarter note value per drum but accent on snare, then goes back 1 number. An example from the table - 1 2 3 4

Drum 1 (LLRR) Drum 2 (LLRR) Drum 1 (**L**)   THEN
Drum 2 (LLRR) Drum 3 (LLRR) Drum 1 (**L**)   THEN
Drum 3 (LLRR) Drum 4 (LLRR) Drum 1 (**L**)

This is a **2** bar pattern

412

Hand Drum Numbers			
1234	2341	3412	4123
1243	2314	3421	4132
1324	2134	3124	4213
1342	2143	3142	4231
1423	2413	3214	4312
1432	2431	3241	4321

Objective - Single Stroke 4 - Left Lead

Single stroke four is based on alternating singles.

<u>CONSIDER THE DYNAMIC LEVELS AS **6** FOR THE ACCENT AND **3** FOR THE UNACCENTED, WITH NO OTHER CHANGE IN VOLUME.</u>

The pattern is L R L **R**

413

Beat of the Week

The drum beat will support all exercises this week. Always use a metronome at the set tempo. Keep an eye on both hands and feet while practicing to develop better technique and effective posture.

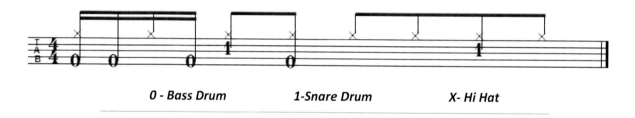

0 - Bass Drum   **1-Snare Drum**   **X- Hi Hat**

Day 1 - Pattern - LRL**R**

Sixteenth Note Triplet Hand Tempo = 54 (+8)

TIMING - SIXTEENTH NOTES TRIPLET - COUNTED AS - 1 TRIP LET AND TRIP LET 2 TRIP LET AND TRIP LET 3 TRIP LET AND TRIP LET 4 TRIP LET AND TRIP LET

GUIDE

									Sixteenth Note triplet Count														
1	Trip	Let	And	Trip	Let	2	Trip	Let	And	Trip	Let	3	Trip	Let	And	Trip	Let	4	Trip	Let	And	Trip	Let
L	R	L	R			L	R	L	R			L	R	L	R			L	R	L	R		

ACCENTS ARE IN BOLD

Day 2 - Pattern - LRL**R**

Sixteenth Note Triplet Feet Tempo = 34 (+8)

<u>Timing - Sixteenth Notes Triplet - Counted as - 1 Trip Let and Trip Let 2 Trip Let and Trip Let 3 Trip Let and Trip Let 4 Trip Let and Trip Let</u>

<u>Guide</u>

Sixteenth Note triplet Count																							
1	Trip	Let	And	Trip	Let	2	Trip	Let	And	Trip	Let	3	Trip	Let	And	Trip	Let	4	Trip	Let	And	Trip	Let
L	R	L	R			L	R	L	**R**			L	R	L	**R**			L	R	L	**R**		

<u>Accents are in bold</u>

416

Day 3 - Pattern - LRL**R**

Full Hand Pattern Applied to Drum Numbers Tempo = 54 (+8)

TIMING - SIXTEENTH NOTES TRIPLET - COUNTED AS - 1 TRIP LET AND TRIP LET 2 TRIP LET AND TRIP LET 3 TRIP LET AND TRIP LET 4 TRIP LET AND TRIP LET

GUIDE

Hand application, an example from the table - 3 4 1 2

Drum 3 (LRL**R**), Drum 4 (LRL**R**), Drum 1 (LRL**R**), Drum 2(LRL**R**)

THIS IS A **1** BAR PATTERN

Hand Drum Numbers			
1234	2341	3412	4123
1243	2314	3421	4132
1324	2134	3124	4213
1342	2143	3142	4231
1423	2413	3214	4312
1432	2431	3241	4321

417

Day 4 -Pattern- LRL**R**

Split Hand + Feet D. Numbers Tempo = 54 (+8)

<u>TIMING - SIXTEENTH NOTES TRIPLET - COUNTED AS - 1 TRIP LET AND TRIP LET 2 TRIP LET AND TRIP LET 3 TRIP LET AND TRIP LET 4 TRIP LET AND TRIP LET</u>

<u>GUIDE</u>

Application,

The first number / letter will be playing represents the R part of the rudiment, whilst the second number / letter will be playing represents the L part of the rudiment.

Drum Numbers			
Split Limbs		**Abbreviation Guide**	
O	LH	0	Bass Drum
RH	O	RH	Right Hand
Y	RH	Y	Left Foot
LH	Y	LH	Left Hand
O	RH		
RH	Y		
Y	LH		
LH	O		

Day 5 - Pattern - LRL**R**

Hand Pattern Applied to DN, Accent On Snare Tempo = 54 (+8)

TIMING - SIXTEENTH NOTES TRIPLET - COUNTED AS - 1 TRIP LET AND TRIP LET 2 TRIP LET AND TRIP LET 3 TRIP LET AND TRIP LET 4 TRIP LET AND TRIP LET

GUIDE

The aim of this exercise is to play the accents on the snare drum. The unaccented notes will follow the drum numbers according to day 3 .

Maintain Accent always

Hand Drum Numbers			
1234	2341	3412	4123
1243	2314	3421	4132
1324	2134	3124	4213
1342	2143	3142	4231
1423	2413	3214	4312
1432	2431	3241	4321

Day 6 - Pattern - LRL**R**

Sixteenth Note Triplet Hand Tempo = 54 (+8)

<u>Timing - Sixteenth Notes Triplet - Counted as - 1 Trip Let and Trip Let 2 Trip Let and Trip Let 3 Trip Let and Trip Let 4 Trip Let and Trip Let</u>

<u>Guide</u>

									Sixteenth Note triplet Count														
1	Trip	Let	And	Trip	Let	2	Trip	Let	And	Trip	Let	3	Trip	Let	And	Trip	Let	4	Trip	Let	And	Trip	Let
L	R	L	**R**	0	0	L	R	L	**R**	0	0	L	R	L	**R**	0	0	L	R	L	**R**	0	0

<u>Once comfortable, apply to drum numbers according to Day 3 first then Day 5</u>

<u>Accents are in bold</u>

Day 7 - Pattern - LRL**R**

Sixteenth Note Triplet Hand Tempo = 54 (+8)

TIMING - SIXTEENTH NOTES TRIPLET - COUNTED AS - 1 TRIP LET AND TRIP LET 2 TRIP LET AND TRIP LET 3 TRIP LET AND TRIP LET 4 TRIP LET AND TRIP LET

GUIDE

										Sixteenth Note triplet Count												
1	Trip	Let	And	Trip	Let	2	Trip	Let	And	Trip	Let	3	Trip	Let	And	Trip	Let	4	Trip	Let	And	Trip	Let
0	0	L	R	L	**R**	0	0	L	R	L	**R**	0	0	L	R	L	**R**	0	0	L	R	L	**R**

ONCE COMFORTABLE, APPLY TO DRUM NUMBERS ACCORDING TO DAY 3 FIRST THEN DAY 5

ACCENTS ARE IN BOLD

Objective-Freestyle Mix of Past Rudiments

Mix all the various exercises we have learnt into a variety of combinations as follows, using daily application method daily.

Day	Rudiments To Mix	Daily Application Method
1	Single Stroke 7 + Flam Paradiddle	Hands
2	11 Stroke Roll + Inverted Paradiddle 3	Feet
3	15 Stroke Roll + Swiss Army Triplet	Split Limbs
4	Single Dragadiddle + 6 Stroke Roll	Across Drum Numbers
5	Flamacue + Single Stroke 4	Accent Across Drum Numbers
6	Triple Ratamacue + 9 Stroke Roll	Accent On Snare Drum
7	Drag Paradiddle #1 + Lesson 25	Across Cymbals

Keep an eye on both hands and feet while practicing to develop better technique.

Objective - Triple Paradiddle - Right Lead

Triple paradiddle is 6 alternating single notes followed by a double / diddle.

CONSIDER THE DYNAMIC LEVELS AS 6 FOR THE ACCENT AND 3 FOR THE UNACCENTED, WITH NO OTHER CHANGE IN VOLUME.

The pattern is **R** L R L R L R R **L** R L R L R L L

Beat of the Week

The drum beat will support all exercises this week. Always use a metronome at the set tempo. Keep an eye on both hands and feet while practicing to develop better technique and effective posture.

0 - Bass Drum   **1-Snare Drum**   **X- Hi Hat**

Day 1 - Pattern - **R**LRLRLRR **L**RLRLRLL

Sixteenth Note Hand Tempo = 54 (+8)

TIMING - SIXTEENTH NOTES - COUNTED AS 1E &D 2 E & D 3 E & D 4 E & D

GUIDE

Sixteenth Note Count Applied															
1	E	&	D	2	E	&	D	3	E	&	D	4	E	&	D
R	L	R	L	R	L	R	R	L	R	L	R	L	R	L	L

ACCENT IS ON BEAT 1 AND 3.

Day 2 - Pattern - **R**LRLRLR**R** **L**RLRLR**LL**

Sixteenth Note Feet Tempo = 34 (+8)

TIMING - SIXTEENTH NOTES - COUNTED AS 1E &D 2 E & D 3 E & D 4 E & D

GUIDE

Sixteenth Note Count Applied															
1	E	&	D	2	E	&	D	**3**	E	&	D	4	E	&	D
R	L	R	L	R	L	R	R	**L**	R	L	R	L	R	L	L

ACCENT IS ON BEAT 1 AND 3.

Day 3 - Pattern - **R**LRLRLRR **L**RLRLRLL

Split Hand Pattern Applied to Drum Numbers Tempo = 54 (+8)

TIMING - SIXTEENTH NOTES - COUNTED AS 1E &D 2 E & D 3 E & D 4 E & D

GUIDE

Quarter note value per drum

An example from the table - 3 4 1 2

Drum 3 (**R**LRL) Drum 4 (RLRR) Drum 1 (**L**RLR) Drum 2 (LRLL)

THIS IS A **1** BAR PATTERN

Hand Drum Numbers			
1234	2341	3412	4123
1243	2314	3421	4132
1324	2134	3124	4213
1342	2143	3142	4231
1423	2413	3214	4312
1432	2431	3241	4321

Day 4 - Pattern - **R**LRLRLRR **L**RLRLRLL

Split Hand + Feet D. Numbers Tempo = 54 (+8)
TIMING - SIXTEENTH NOTES - COUNTED AS 1E &D 2 E & D 3 E & D 4 E & D

GUIDE

Application,

The first number / letter will be playing represents the R part of the rudiment, whilst the second number / letter will be playing represents the L part of the rudiment.

Drum Numbers			
Split Limbs		**Abbreviation Guide**	
O	LH	0	Bass Drum
RH	O	RH	Right Hand
Y	RH	Y	Left Foot
LH	Y	LH	Left Hand
O	RH		
RH	Y		
Y	LH		
LH	O		

Day 5 - Pattern - **R**LRLRLRR **L**RLRLRLL

Pattern as a Beat Tempo = 54 (+8)

TIMING - SIXTEENTH NOTES - COUNTED AS 1E &D 2 E & D 3 E & D 4 E & D

GUIDE

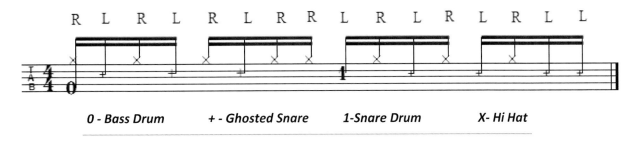

0 - Bass Drum   + - Ghosted Snare   1-Snare Drum   X- Hi Hat

ACCENT IS ON THE 'AND' OF EACH QUARTER NOTE

Day 6 - Pattern - **R**LRLRLRR **L**RLRLRLL

Eighth Note Triplet Hand Tempo = 54 (+8)

TIMING - EIGHTH NOTE TRIPLET - COUNTED AS 1 TRIP LET 2 TRIP LET 3 TRIP LET 4 TRIP LET

GUIDE

Eighth Note triplet Count												
1	Trip	Let	2	Trip	Let	3	Trip	Let	4	Trip	Let
R	L	R	L	R	L	R	R				
L	R	L	R	L	R	L	L				

BASS DRUM SHOULD PLAY STEADY QUARTER NOTES. THIS IS A **2** BAR PATTERN.

ONCE YOU ARE COMFORTABLE WITH THE EXERCISE, APPLY TO DRUM NUMBERS ACROSS THE KIT

Day 7 - Pattern - **R**LRLRLRR **L**RLRLRLL

Eighth Note Triplet Feet Tempo = 44 (+8)

TIMING - EIGHTH NOTE TRIPLET - COUNTED AS 1 TRIP LET 2 TRIP LET 3 TRIP LET 4 TRIP LET

GUIDE

Eighth Note triplet Count											
1	Trip	Let	2	Trip	Let	3	Trip	Let	4	Trip	Let
R	L	R	L	R	L	R	R				
L	R	L	R	L	R	L	L				

THIS IS A **2** BAR PATTERN

Objective-Freestyle Mix of Past Rudiments

Mix all the various exercises we have learnt into a variety of combinations as follows, using daily application method daily.

Day	Rudiments To Mix	Daily Application Method
1	Triple Paradiddle + Single Stroke 7	Hands
2	Inverted Paradiddle #3 + Drag Tap	Feet
3	Flam Tap + Lesson 25	Split Limbs
4	Five Stroke Roll + Double Paradiddle	Across Drum Numbers
5	9 Stroke Roll + Flam	Accent Across Drum Numbers
6	Flam Accent + 11 Stroke Roll	Accent On Snare Drum
7	Flam Paradiddle + Single Stroke 4	Across Cymbals

Keep an eye on both hands and feet while practicing to develop better technique.

Objective-Freestyle Mix of Past Rudiments

Mix all the various exercises we have learnt into a variety of combinations as follows, using daily application method daily.

Day	Rudiments To Mix	Daily Application Method
1	Drag Paradiddle + Triple Paradiddle	Hands
2	Paradiddle + Drag Tap	Feet
3	Paradiddle + Triple Stroke Roll	Split Limbs
4	Flam Tap + Flamacue	Across Drum Numbers
5	Single Drag Tap + Swiss Army Triplet	Accent Across Drum Numbers
6	Double Stroke Roll + Ratamacue	Accent On Snare Drum
7	Single Stroke Roll + Double Ratamacue	Across Cymbals

Keep an eye on both hands and feet while practicing to develop better technique.

Objective - Drag Paradiddle #2

Drag paradiddle #2 is two accented notes followed by a paradiddle, with drag grace notes on the second accented note and the first note of the paradiddle.   This is an alternating rudiment.

CONSIDER THE DYNAMIC LEVELS AS **6** FOR THE ACCENT AND **3** FOR THE UNACCENTED, WITH NO OTHER CHANGE IN VOLUME.

The pattern is **R** llR llR L R R   **L** rrL rrL R L L

434

Beat of the Week

The drum beat will support all exercises this week. Always use a metronome at the set tempo. Keep an eye on both hands and feet while practicing to develop better technique and effective posture.

0 - Bass Drum   *1-Snare Drum*   *X- Hi Hat*

Day 1-Pattern-**R** llR llR L RR - **L** rrL rrL R LL

Sixteenth Note Hand Tempo = 54 (+8)

TIMING - SIXTEENTH NOTES - COUNTED AS 1E &D 2 E & D 3 E & D 4 E & D

GUIDE

Sixteenth Note Count Applied															
1	E	&	D	2	E	&	D	**3**	E	&	D	4	E	&	D
R		llR		llR	L	R	R	**L**		rrL		rrL	R	L	L

ACCENT IS ON BEAT 1 AND 3.

Day 2-Pattern-**R** llR llR L RR - **L** rrL rrL R LL

Sixteenth Note Feet Tempo = 34 (+8)

TIMING - SIXTEENTH NOTES - COUNTED AS 1E &D 2 E & D 3 E & D 4 E & D

GUIDE

Sixteenth Note Count Applied															
1	E	&	D	2	E	&	D	**3**	E	&	D	4	E	&	D
R		llR		llR	L	R	R	**L**		rrL		rrL	R	L	L

ACCENT IS ON BEAT 1 AND 3.

Day 3 -Pattern-**R** llR llR L RR - **L** rrL rrL R LL

Split Hand D. Numbers Tempo = 54 (+8)

TIMING - SIXTEENTH NOTES - COUNTED AS 1E &D 2 E & D 3 E & D 4 E & D

GUIDE

Hand application, an example from the table - 3 4

Left hand remains on the first number (**3**), whilst Right hand remains on the second number (**4**).

BASS DRUM SHOULD HAVE STEADY QUARTER NOTE PULSE.

Drum Numbers			
12	23	32	41
13	24	34	42
14	21	31	43
1X	2X	3X	4X

Day 4-Pattern-**R** llR llR L RR - **L** rrL rrL R LL

Hand Pattern Applied to Drum Numbers Tempo = 54 (+8)

TIMING - SIXTEENTH NOTES - COUNTED AS 1E &D 2 E & D 3 E & D 4 E & D

GUIDE

Quarter note value per drum

An example from the table - 3 4 1 2

    Drum 3 (**R** llR) Drum 4 (llRLRR) Drum 1 (L rrL) Drum 2 (rrLRLL)

THIS IS A **1** BAR PATTERN

Hand Drum Numbers			
1234	2341	3412	4123
1243	2314	3421	4132
1324	2134	3124	4213
1342	2143	3142	4231
1423	2413	3214	4312
1432	2431	3241	4321

Day 5 -Pattern-**R** llR llR L RR - **L** rrL rrL R LL

Hand Pattern Applied to DN, Accent On Snare Tempo = 54 (+8)
TIMING - SIXTEENTH NOTES - COUNTED AS 1E &D 2 E & D 3 E & D 4 E & D

GUIDE

The aim of this exercise is to play the accents only on the Snare drum. The unaccented notes will follow the drum numbers according to day 4 .

Maintain Accent always

Hand Drum Numbers			
1234	2341	3412	4123
1243	2314	3421	4132
1324	2134	3124	4213
1342	2143	3142	4231
1423	2413	3214	4312
1432	2431	3241	4321

Day 6 -Pattern-**R** llR llR L RR - **L** rrL rrL R LL

Hand Accents Applied to Drum Numbers Tempo = 54 (+8)

TIMING - SIXTEENTH NOTES - COUNTED AS 1E &D 2 E & D 3 E & D 4 E & D

GUIDE

The pattern **R** llR llR L RR - **L** rrL rrL R LL is played on the hi-hat or any drum including snare drum. However, every accent to be played, should be played according to the drum numbers.

PLAY NOTES AS CLOSE TOGETHER AS POSSIBLE, BASS DRUM PLAYING ALL QUARTER NOTES.

Hand Drum Numbers			
1234	2341	3412	4123
1243	2314	3421	4132
1324	2134	3124	4213
1342	2143	3142	4231
1423	2413	3214	4312
1432	2431	3241	4321

Day 7 -Pattern-**R** llR llR L RR - **L** rrL rrL R LL

Cymbal Tempo = 54 (+8)

TIMING - SIXTEENTH NOTES - COUNTED AS 1E &D 2 E & D 3 E & D 4 E & D

GUIDE

Play the drag paradiddle #2 pattern on one crash cymbal or multiple cymbals, maintaining accents on beats 1 + 3.

The pattern can be played as normal for multiple bars to build ambience in a ballad song or at the end.

Try the pattern with and without the bass drum for a variation of effects.

Objective - Paradiddle - Left Lead

A paradiddle consists of two single strokes followed by a double stroke, i.e., RLRR or LRLL. When multiple paradiddles are played in succession, the first note being accented always alternates between right and left limbs. Therefore, a single paradiddle is often used to switch the "lead hand" in drumming.

<u>CONSIDER THE DYNAMIC LEVELS AS **6** FOR THE ACCENT AND **3** FOR THE UNACCENTED, WITH NO OTHER CHANGE IN VOLUME.</u>

The pattern is **L** R L L **R** L R R

Beat of the Week

The drum beat will support all exercises this week. Always use a metronome at the set tempo. Keep an eye on both hands and feet while practicing to develop better technique and effective posture.

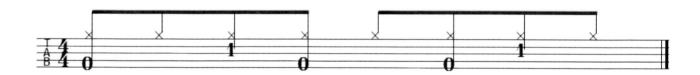

0 - Bass Drum   **1-Snare Drum**   **X- Hi Hat**

Day 1-Pattern - **L** R L L - **R** L R R

Sixteenth Note Hand Tempo = 54 (+8)

TIMING - SIXTEENTH NOTES - COUNTED AS 1E &D 2 E & D 3 E & D 4 E & D

GUIDE

Sixteenth Note Count Applied															
1	E	&	D	**2**	E	&	D	**3**	E	&	D	**4**	E	&	D
L	R	L	L	**R**	L	R	R	**L**	R	L	L	**R**	L	R	R

ACCENT IS ON EACH QUARTER NOTES.

Day 2-Pattern - **L** R L L - **R** L R R

Sixteenth Note Feet Tempo = 34 (+8)

TIMING - SIXTEENTH NOTES - COUNTED AS 1E &D 2 E & D 3 E & D 4 E & D

GUIDE

Sixteenth Note Count Applied															
1	E	&	D	2	E	&	D	3	E	&	D	4	E	&	D
L	R	L	L	R	L	R	R	L	R	L	L	R	L	R	R

ACCENT IS ON EACH QUARTER NOTES.

Day 3 - Pattern - **L** R L L - **R** L R R

Hand Pattern Applied to Drum Numbers Tempo = 54 (+8)

TIMING - SIXTEENTH NOTES - COUNTED AS 1E &D 2 E & D 3 E & D 4 E & D

GUIDE

Quarter note value per drum

An example from the table - 3 4 1 2

Drum 3 (**L**RLL) Drum 4 (**R**LRR) Drum 1 (**L**RLL) Drum 2 (**R**LRR)

THIS IS A **1** BAR PATTERN

Hand Drum Numbers			
1234	2341	3412	4123
1243	2314	3421	4132
1324	2134	3124	4213
1342	2143	3142	4231
1423	2413	3214	4312
1432	2431	3241	4321

Day 4 - Pattern - **L** R L L - **R** L R R

Split Hand + Feet D. Numbers Tempo = 54 (+8)

<u>TIMING - SIXTEENTH NOTES - COUNTED AS 1E &D 2 E & D 3 E & D 4 E & D</u>

<u>GUIDE</u>

Application,

The first number / letter will be playing represents the R part of the rudiment, whilst the second number / letter will be playing represents the L part of the rudiment.

Drum Numbers			
Split Limbs		Abbreviation Guide	
O	LH	O	Bass Drum
RH	O	RH	Right Hand
Y	RH	Y	Left Foot
LH	Y	LH	Left Hand
O	RH		
RH	Y		
Y	LH		
LH	O		

Day 5 - Pattern - **L** R L L - **R** L R R

Split Hand D.Numbers Tempo = 54 (+8)
TIMING - SIXTEENTH NOTES - COUNTED AS 1E &D 2 E & D 3 E & D 4 E & D

GUIDE

Hand application, an example from the table - 3 4

Left hand remains on the first number **(3)**, whilst Right hand remains on the second number **(4)**.

BASS DRUM SHOULD HAVE STEADY QUARTER NOTE PULSE.

Drum Numbers			
12	23	32	41
13	24	34	42
14	21	31	43
1X	2X	3X	4X

Day 6 - Pattern - **L** R L L - **R** L R R

Pattern as a Beat Tempo = 54 (+8)

TIMING - SIXTEENTH NOTES - COUNTED AS 1E &D 2 E & D 3 E & D 4 E & D

GUIDE

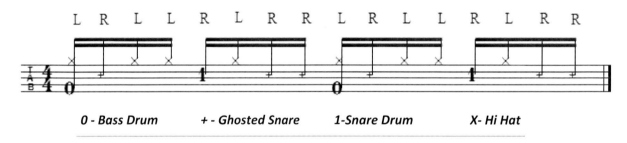

0 - Bass Drum   *+ - Ghosted Snare*   *1-Snare Drum*   *X- Hi Hat*

ACCENT IS ON EACH QUARTER NOTES

Day 7 - Pattern - **L** R L L - **R** L R R

Pattern as a Beat Tempo = 54 (+8)

TIMING - SIXTEENTH NOTES - COUNTED AS 1E &D 2 E & D 3 E & D 4 E & D

GUIDE

Similar to day 6 but with the RIGHT HAND pattern following the drum numbers and accent on the snare drum. .

Maintain Accent always

Hand Drum Numbers			
1234	2341	3412	4123
1243	2314	3421	4132
1324	2134	3124	4213
1342	2143	3142	4231
1423	2413	3214	4312
1432	2431	3241	4321

Objective-Freestyle Mix of Past Rudiments

Mix all the various exercises we have learnt into a variety of combinations as follows, using daily application method daily.

Day	Rudiments To Mix	Daily Application Method
1	Pataflafla + Lesson 25	Hands
2	Single Stroke 7 + Flam Accent	Feet
3	Inverted Paradiddle + Swiss Army Triplet	Split Limbs
4	Single Stroke 4 + Inverted Flam Tap	Across Drum Numbers
5	Inverted Double + 6 Stroke Roll	Accent Across Drum Numbers
6	17 Stroke Roll + Flam Accent	Accent On Snare Drum
7	Drag Paradiddle + Paradiddle	Across Cymbals

Keep an eye on both hands and feet while practicing to develop better technique.

Progress Record			
Rudiment	Year 1 Tempo	Year 2 Tempo	Year 3 Tempo
Week 1 - Single Stroke Roll			
W eek 2 - Double Stroke Roll			
Week 3 - Paradiddle			
Week 4 - Five Stroke Roll			
Week 5 - Double Stroke Roll			
Week 6 - Inverted Double Stroke 1			
Week 7 - Single Stroke 4			
Week 8 - Single Stroke 7			
Week 9 - 10 Stroke Roll			
Week 10 - Inverted Paradiddle #1			
Week 11 - Inverted Paradiddle #2			
Week 12 - Drag			
Week 13 - Pataflafla			
Week 14 - Freestyle Rudiments			
Week 15 - Five Stroke Roll			
Week 16 - Single Ratamacue			
Week 17 - Flam Drag			

Week 18 - Flam			
Week 19 - Multiple Bounce Roll			
Week 20 - Flam accent			
Week 21 - Triple Stroke Roll			
Week 22 - Single Drag Tap			
Week 23 - Seventeen Stroke Roll			
Week 24 - Flam Tap			
Week 25 - Double Ratamacue			
Week 26 - Freestyle Rudiments			
Week 27 - Single Stroke 7			
Week 28 - Flam Paradiddle			
Week 29 - Eleven Stroke Roll			
Week 30 - Fifteen Stroke Roll			
Week 31 - Freestyle Rudiments			
Week 32 - Seven Stroke Roll			
Week 33 - Single Dragadiddle			
Week 34 - Swiss Army Triplet			
Week 35 - Double Drag Tap			
Week 36 - Six Stroke Roll			

Week 37 - Lesson 25			
Week 38 - Double Paradiddle			
Week 39 - Drag Paradiddle #1			
Week 40 - Inverted Flam Tap			
Week 41 - Thirteen Stroke Roll			
Week 42 - Triple Ratamacue			
Week 43 - Flamacue			
Week 44 - Inverted Double Stroke #1			
Week 45 - Nine Stroke Roll			
Week 46 - Single Stroke Four			
Week 47 - Freestyle Rudiments			
Week 48 - Triple Paradiddle			
Week 49 - Freestyle Rudiments			
Week 50 - Freestyle Rudiments			
Week 51 - Drag Paradiddle #2			
Week 52 - Paradiddle			
Week 53 - Freestyle Rudiments			